Conversations with the Rebbe

CONVERSATIONS

With The Rebbe
MENACHEM MENDEL
SCHNEERSON

Interviews with 14 leading figures about the Rebbe

Herman Branover
Herb Brin
Shoshana Cardin
Zalman Dimetrofsky
David Hollander
Malcolm Hoenlein
Norman Lamm
Nathan Lewin
Nissen Mangel
Menachem Porush
Chaim Potok
Yitzchok Shamir
Abraham Twerski
Herbert Weiner

Interviewed By CHAIM DALFIN

JEC PUBLISHING COMPANY, INC. / LOS ANGELES

Library of Congress Cataloging-in-Publication Data

Dalfin, Chaim
Conversations with the Rebbe / Interviews / Menachem Mendel Schneerson / Chaim Dalfin

p. cm.
"I have asked them to share their conversations, meetings, and correspondence with the Rebbe over the course of the last fifty years. In this book Jewish personalities speak for themselves." - Introduction.

ISBN 1-880880-16-4

1. Chasidism 2. Chabad 3. Judaism-Interviews I. Schneerson, Menachem Mendel, 1902-1994. II. Title III. Chaim Dalfin
1996

Printed in the United States of America

First Edition

1 2 3 4 5 6 7 8 9 10

BOOK DESIGN BY OFRA SHIPMAN

DEDICATION

Dear Rebbe...
we miss you, we need you, we want you, we love you
we know your coming back very soon...

CONTENTS

vii

CONTENTS

INTRODUCTION

Rabbi Menachem Mendel Schneerson, the seventh Rebbe of the Chabad-Lubavitch movement, was not only a leader for his own followers. He was a leader for all of mankind. Just as Moses was a leader for all of humanity, so to, this Rebbe. As we find in the writings of the Zohar, the classical Kabbalistic text, in every generation there lives a Moses. The soul of Moses is manifest in the leader of the generation.

This is my point of view. I am a product of Lubavitch Yeshivos, a Shliach of the Rebbe who has been attempting to carry out his will for my entire adult life. But the Rebbe has never limited himself to his followers. He has reached out directly to every Jew he can. Therefore there is a need to gather up the memories of this contact in order that all of those who find themselves in similar positions may learn from him. As the Rebbe has said many times, in the name of the Tzemach Tzedek, "What is printed is for all generations."

The only question was where to start. In this work, I have chosen public people; leaders of Jewish organizations, writers whose work has reached millions, rabbis in influential posts. They speak both for themselves and their followers. I have asked them to share with us their conversations, meetings, and correspondence with the Rebbe over the course of the last fifty years.

It is people who are in leadership positions whose words make a difference. People pay attention to them because they express the ideals current in society. Therefore I went around the world interviewing these people. I feel it is their words that will tell the world about the who and what the Rebbe is. Through their personal experiences, people will have a chance to hear and learn from them about the Rebbe.

The Rebbe was a visionary. He saw the future not just in spiritual terms but in very practical ways. He therefore acted upon his vision in a constructive manner. Not only did he himself get involved but he encouraged others to do the same. His words revealed out their inner strength. He didn't speak *at* them, but *with* them. Whether it was a President of the United States or a blue collar worker, the Rebbe was able to see the potential each individual had, and, even more so, to bring out that quality in the person.

The Rebbe was also a communicator. His message didn't remain aloof, abstract and esoteric. He communicated the most sophisticated and crucial information in the most simple, down-to-earth way. Yet he didn't compromise one iota on the message. The kernel of truth permeated every message. Be it to children, adults, senior citizens, college students — the Rebbe's words made an impact. For he truly knew how to communicate. The Rebbe's messages were all fueled by a common element: sincerity. As the saying goes, "words coming from the heart, enter the other persons heart." Because of his sincerity, the Rebbe was able to reach the talmudic scholar and the preschool child alike.

It is difficult to overcome the loss of a good friend. It is even more difficult to overcome the loss of a parent. However, in a sense, it is most difficult to overcome the loss of the mentor who formed and shaped one's outlook in life. We all are here for a purpose. It isn't just to have fun. We are here to carry out G-d's purpose in creation, with joy and good will. We are here to share with others those ideals that we have learned from great people. Every individual is a complete world, and every individual has a world in which he lives and which he can influence.

I miss our Rebbe greatly. However, I know that the only way for us to overcome the physical loss, is to realize that the Rebbe continues his work. As the Talmud tells us about Moshe Rabbeinu, "Just as he stood and served before, he stands and serves now." I know that he intercedes from on high on our behalf and brings goodness and happiness into our lives. It is this spirituality that becomes reality. One realizes that one is able to connect with the Rebbe's words and directives in a way that was not possible while he was physically alive. There are no more limitations of time and space. His essence is communicated in his writings and teachings. It's available to you, honored readers. All you have to do is allow yourself the opportunity to "drink from the fountain."

In this book, Jewish personalities speak for themselves. Of course, I do not agree with everything and everyone. This work can be read at three different levels. First, it is an insight into the life and work of the activists of our generation. When they talk about the Rebbe, they reveal themselves. "What Shimon says about Reuven can tell you more about Shimon than it tells about Reuven." Here is a chance to enter the living rooms of some of our most famous personalities. For that reason I have preserved many of the Yiddish and Hebrew turns of phrase which they may not use in their public statements.

Second, it gives insight into the relationship between the Rebbe and those who came in contact with him. It is a lesson in Ahavas Yisroel, in the way one Jew can help and influence others who do not agree with him, follow his lifestyle, or move in the same circles. The way the Rebbe has combined warmth and tolerance with unswerving devotion to truth is a lesson for everyone. This combination is the strength which has made the Chabad movement a force to be reckoned with.

Third, we are privileged to interact once again with the Rebbe himself and his Torah, in a very special way. The Ethics of the Fathers teach that "Whoever says a thing in the name of the one who said it brings Redemption to the world." Although most of the interviews themselves do not stress the themes of Moshiach and Geulah, each of the interviewees has made an important contribution: they acknowledge and permit the publication of the Rebbe's words, "the worldly conversations of a Torah scholar", which are also Torah. In this merit, may we all momentarily see, with our physical eyes, the true and perfect Redemption through our righteous Moshiach.

Rabbi Chaim Dalfin
Los Angeles

BIOGRAPHY

RABBI MENACHEM MENDEL SCHNEERSON

(1902 - 1994)

Rabbi Menachem Mendel Schneerson, the seventh Rebbe of the Chabad-Lubavitch movement, was born on April 18, 1902 in Nikolayev, a town in the Southern Ukraine. In 1928 he married the previous Lubavitcher Rebbe's second-eldest daughter, Chaya Mushka. This drew Rabbi Menachem Mendel into the inner circle of the Chabad-Lubavitch Chasidus. He then began studying mathematics and science at the University of Berlin. In 1933, because of the Nazi rise, he left Berlin for Paris. There he continued his studies at the Sorbonne. When the Nazis occupied Paris, he escaped the city. Rabbi Menachem Mendel and his wife arrived by boat in New York on June 23, 1941. There he met up with his father-in-law, who appointed him as the head of Chabad-Lubavitch's educational division.

In 1950, the previous Rebbe passed away. A year later, Rabbi Menachem Mendel took over the leadership of the Chabad-Lubavitch movement. Over the course of the next forty-four years, the Rebbe developed the small, nearly decimated group of Lubavitch chasidim, to a world-wide community of several hundreds of thousands. Today there are more than two thousand Chabad-Lubavitch institutions in thirty-five countries on six continents. In 1992, at the age of ninety, the Rebbe suffered a stroke; he passed away two years later, on June 12, 1994.

ACKNOWLEDGEMENTS

When one wants to thank people for their assistance, one realizes how insufficient the thanks are. Whatever one can say will only express a glimpse of the true and deep feelings of the heart. To all those who gave of themselves to help spread the ideals of Torah and Mitzvos, the true thanks will come from G-d Almighty who is limitless and infinite. It is G-d who truly "pays back" and whose blessing truly means something.

To begin with, I say thanks to G-d, who gave me the strength to persevere in this work. It is G-d who gives strength. All He asks, is that we allow His blessing to enter. Fortunate are those who make themselves a "keli", a vessel, to receive and to acknowledge that it all comes from Him.

I wish for each and every one who assisted in the book becoming a reality, that G-d's Brocha, which is infinite, be bestowed upon you and your families. I do want to mention several people in particular for special recognition.

First is our dear and beloved Rebbe, Menachem Mendel Schneerson, whose teachings and directives are alive now, more than before. The Rebbe did not just leave us a legacy; he lives on through the study and practice of his teachings. As a student and chasid, I merited to share His holiness with all the interviewees.

Special thanks go to my parents, Reb Aron Hillel and Miriam Dalfin, who gave me my foundation and continue to strengthen it; my dear wife, Bashi who allowed me to travel worldwide to gather the interviews; my five children, Menachem Mendel, Shterna Sara, Brocha, Hinda Fraida, and Chaya Mushka who constantly kept me on my feet, making the combination of writing and family responsibilities a real test, which all of us are better for; my brother Anshel, my good friend Yossi, both of who continue to support my endeavors; my paternal grandparents of blessed memory, Reb Shlomo and Baila Dalfin, and my maternal grandparents of blessed memory, Reb Shlomo Menashe and Hinda Fraida Wiroslow, who were living examples of commitment to Hashem. May this book contribute to the eternal bliss that they experience in the world of truth.

I express my appreciation to Mr. Avrohom Modes, who transcribed the interviews and edited the manuscript using his vast background of Jewish and general studies. May G-d grant you health, happiness, and spiritual growth. My deepest thanks to Mrs. Ofra Shipman for designing my book cover, and to Bryan Ellison for the late hours spent on valuable corrections. Finally, I thank all those who their names escape me. May each and every one of you be blessed.

May this book be received and viewed as a stepping stone toward the fulfillment of the Rebbe's reality, the revelation of Moshiach Now! As the Rebbe said, "Open your eyes and you will see him," Amen!

INTERVIEWS

Professor Herman Branover

World Renowned Scientist Beersheva University,
Founder SATEC Industrial Company

CHASIDIC SCIENTIST

CD   *Professor Branover, your known as a world renowned scientist, a Refusenik and a chasid. Can you describe the history of your path, your parents? What was it within you that got you searching for Yiddishkeit?*

HB   I was born in Riga, Latvia in 1931. My education was mainly in Leningrad, now called Petersberg. I went back to Riga for the summers. My family was absolutely assimilated. My father was an atheist. He was killed right after the beginning of the Second World War, in 1941.

My grandfather used to take me to shul for Rosh Hashanah and Yom Kippur, Pesach, that's all. I really had no exposure. There was no such thing as conservative and reform, but the house wasn't kosher. He wouldn't let pork into the house, he tried not to actually work on Shabbos, but the fine points weren't there. In his childhood he attended a Talmud Torah. I was educated in Soviet schools and Soviet University, so I was also atheistic. I began my search for G-d when one day I was beaten up in the street, I was treated to all kinds of unpleasant words, and I suddenly felt that I was different. I couldn't make peace with the fact that I am different and therefore I have to suffer. There had to be a reason why.

It was 1948 and I had just become a student and the anti-Semitism was intense under Stalin. I wanted to know why I was treated so badly. For many years I couldn't find an answer. If someone knew, they wouldn't tell, for fear of Siberia or something worse than Siberia. I studied by myself. I found a Siddur with Russian translation, so old-fashioned I couldn't understand the Russian.

As time went on I was involved in sensitive research, including military. In those circles it was very dangerous to be curious about Judaism, even though it was fifteen years after Stalin. This was the 60's and it was Brezhnev.

I started going to shul on Shabbos morning. There is one shul in Riga which had survived Hitler and Stalin. There was an upstairs shul, and in the basement, Chasidism davened. I went to the Chasidism, not because I had the slightest idea of what it meant, but because I felt safer, with less chance of being seen. One Shabbos morning I got a visitor in my corner of the shul, and he scared me to death because he told me he knows I am interested in Yiddishkeit. That was the first Chabad Chasid I met.

Later I went to his home, and I started for myself a new world. He surprised me with all kinds of discourses about space and time and how G-d created the world, and how G-d is beyond time and space, and I was sure this man is a physicist, because he speaks about Einstein's theory of relativity. Then he explained to me what the practical Mitzvos are. He literally forced me to put on Tefillin. Although I had searched for Yiddishkeit for many years, I was not prepared for such material things.

The Chasidism researched me. It was months and months before they let me into a Farbrengen. Then I found out about the Rebbe. I learned a Sichah. It was handwritten. A printed Sichah could not go through the mail, so someone in Kfar Chabad [Israel] wrote it out as a personal letter. They began it with some personal remarks, and then came the material. They continued this way in the subsequent "letters".

Then I learned about the history of the thirties in Russia. I couldn't imagine that anyone had ever run a school, a Yeshiva, under Stalin. It was worse than death, but they not only made schools, they did fundraising in a completely silent way. I myself was involved later. We went to stores, to the public market. All we could say was, "We need money for something Jewish." We couldn't disclose anything. Surprisingly, people gave.

I was involved in Chabad for the last eight years before I left Russia. After I started applying for my exit visa, around 1969-70, they kicked me out of the Academy [Soviet Academy of Sciences], I was jobless, hungry. I started protesting, so they decided to put me in prison.

At a certain stage, in 1972, I felt I could not suffer more. I had just been released from jail, and was expecting to be arrested again. I decided that I had to call the Rebbe himself. I shared the idea of calling the Rebbe with my friends. I couldn't call from home, because my line was cut off by the KGB, so I had to go to the Post Office.

They told me I was crazy. First, no one had ever done it. Second, I would never get a connection, and third, if I do get one they will arrest me on the spot and that's it.

I was very stubborn. I got through in ten minutes, and I got one of the secretaries on the line. I told him who I was, that I needed to talk to the Rebbe. He said, "The Rebbe doesn't speak on the phone!" I said, "OK, I understand, but I am a special case. I just got out of jail, I am probably going back in soon, and I have to talk to the Rebbe. He ultimately transferred me to Rav Hodakov. Rav Hodakov told me the same thing. I was arguing, and pushing, and suddenly I heard a second voice on the line, who spoke to Hodakov, not to me. "Tell him he already has all the blessings, and he must be sure that he will immediately go out."

Then I started waiting. In the visa office, they told me I had no chance, because I was in military research. Maybe they will let me go when I forget everything I studied. I asked them how many years. They said they didn't know, they had not gotten precise instructions, but their guess was maybe ten years, maybe fifteen.

I waited three weeks. At the end of the third week I got an invitation to a certain office. I went there full of expectations, and I was very, very disappointed, because the same woman as before told me in a very angry voice, "Why are you making noise. I told you, you have to wait ten-fifteen years." She was very angry.

I came home, I didn't know what to say. It was about 3:15 in the afternoon. Five minutes later a messenger came — they couldn't call me because my phone was cut off. He told me to return to the office. I should hurry up because they closed at five.

I rushed over, and the same woman told me with great anger, "The management has decided you can go."

What happened in the meantime. I think they themselves didn't know. I would never be able to figure out what had happened. This was the end of 1972, three weeks after the Rebbe's blessing.

That was the first personal experience with the Rebbe.

Over the years I accumulated dozens of invitations to lecture on science outside the Soviet Union. My managers had always told me to excuse myself for family reasons. Now, after I got to Israel, I wrote back to them and they told me that the invitations still stood, they would be happy to see me.

I applied for the necessary papers to go from Israel to New York. I didn't have to tell anyone the real reason I was going, but I knew it. Soon after, I got my first Yechidus, which lasted two hours.

CD   *What was the subject of the first Yechidus?*

HB   The first Yechidus, first of all, I myself was in kind of a fog. I had seen the Rebbe before at Minchah, and the Rebbe walked by and looked at me. That was the first meeting, really. That already made me tremble and shiver. This Yechidus was late at night, I got in about 1:30 am. I was last, because I was told that since I had come from Russia, the Rebbe didn't want me waiting long.

The amazing thing was that when I entered, the Rebbe gave me such a bright Sholom Aleichem, with such a smile. The feeling was that we had been talking the day before, and the Rebbe was continuing it. I felt that the room was somehow physically full of Ahavas Yisroel, as if I could touch it.

Later on I started to understand better what the Rebbe is, but at the beginning I'm afraid I couldn't figure out what the Rebbe was saying because I was so excited and nervous. He spoke to me in Yiddish. He started asking about dozens, maybe hundreds of families in Russia, everywhere, Russia, Siberia. These were people

I supposedly knew, but the Rebbe wanted to know details, and I knew about only a few. The rest I just recognized the names, I didn't know their family affairs. It ended up with the Rebbe telling me about those families. I was amazed. He was telling me what the husband is doing, what the wife is doing, the ages of the children, what each of the children is interested in, the family problems. It was amazing. I was so confused. I couldn't understand how this, this burst of information, [came from one man's memory]. It was the most phenomenal memory, a computer type of information.

Then I started paying attention to how he was speaking. When he speaks about a certain Jew, a certain woman, a certain child, a certain man, the whole world doesn't exist. The only thing that exists is the Jew about whom the Rebbe is concerned at this moment. I started making comparisons. In Israel they had started shlepping me to all the presidents and prime ministers, and famous writers, and famous this, and I had observed them.

In my memory I compared the way the Rebbe would speak and listen with the way they did it, and immediately I perceived the difference. A politician gives you 5%, 10%. If he is tired, he falls asleep. In most cases he is concerned with his party issues, his personal issues, how to hold on to his seat, and you can sense all this.

With the Rebbe you get unlimited attention. If the Rebbe is speaking about a Jew somewhere in Siberia, the whole world is nonexistent.

Of course I was astounded about how the Rebbe spoke about science, and specifically about my field in science. He was up to date, up to the last issues of specialized journals. Even then I knew something about the Rebbe, but I couldn't imagine him sitting and reading scientific journals. He had better things to do. Nevertheless he was on top of the last word in every science. Also literature, education, and the so-called conflict between Torah and science.

The second Yechidus was also two hours, at the end of this first trip to NY. In the meantime I went to universities, gave lectures. At this Yechidus I had my first special instructions from the Rebbe. I had already been accepted as a full professor at Ben-Gurion and also Tel Aviv universities, as a full professor, but they had no laboratories for magnetohydrodynamics. This field had not been developed in Israel.

CD   *What is magnetohydrodynamics?*

HB   A certain field in physics, very advanced. It deals with astrophysics, stars on galaxies. On earth it is concerned with better and cheaper methods of generating electrical energy and so on.

At any rate, I was sure I would have to change fields, because there was no laboratory. At the second Yechidus the Rebbe inquired about my plans.

I told him I had a few days in America. Tomorrow I had to go to Philadelphia. I was invited by a student organization for Soviet Jewry to give a lecture. The Rebbe said, "Give the lecture, but, being in Philadelphia, don't forget to look up a professor in your field."

I was confused and surprised. I followed the literature, and I knew where the work was being done, Tennessee, California. To the best of my knowledge there was nothing going on in Philadelphia. Of course, I didn't dare to ask, and the Rebbe didn't give any names or places.

When I got to Philadelphia, I was met by Avreml Shemtov. He wanted to know what had gone on in Yechidus, and I mentioned this request. He had contacts at Temple University, so he arranged that at a certain time there would be a seminar by a scientist who had just come from Russia, on magnetohydrodynamics. The plan was, that if there was such a professor, he would come! I gave the seminar, but all the professors of physics told me they enjoyed listening, they understood more or less, but it's not their field.

Then we started searching the University of Pennsylvania, hours and hours but no success. It was completely dark, I had to go to my main lecture. We had one building left to search. Someone told me that he thought that in the next building there was a professor who had just moved from California. His name was Professor Yeh, of Chinese origin, and it seemed to this person that his field was magnetohydrodynamics.

We rushed to the other building, and found this Yeh, who

was locking his door at that moment. He told me that he knew me from my books and articles, he was not in a rush. We talked for a half an hour, it was very amazing. He invited me to go to Stanford university in Palo Alto to present a paper to the All-American Conference in magnetohydrodynamics.

I told him I thanked him very much, but I was soon going to Israel. I wrote to the Rebbe, telling him I had met Professor Yeh and gotten this invitation. The same day, I got his answer, "If your university will allow you [the Rebbe was considerate of every-body], and if El Al will agree to postpone your ticket, it is very important that you stay and go to this conference."

I went to the conference, and I was immediately met by two or three people who introduced themselves as representing the American Navy, The Office of Naval Research, and told me that they had come especially to see me. They wanted to offer me a con-tract.

I explained that I had nothing, no laboratory. At that time I hardly knew what a contract is — in Russia we had no such thing as contracts. They said OK, you have no laboratory, we'll give you money and you can build a laboratory.

That contract was renewed for seven subsequent years! It enabled me to build what today is the most advanced laboratory in the world in this field, magnetohydrodynamics.

It's a real Baal-Shemske story. The Baal Shem Tov would tell someone to find a shoemaker somewhere in Timbuktu and the person would just blindly go there and find him!

CD   *What was the interest of the Office of Naval Research?*

HB   First, I came from Russia. They needed to know what the Russians had accomplished. Secondly, this also applies to power stations on ships. They wanted to utilize my experience.

CD   *Have you ever thought about how the Rebbe knew about this Chinese professor?*

HB   That's the real Baal-Shemske element in it. I have no explanations. Listen, this man had just moved a month earlier from California. I knew about research in California , but Philadelphia no. The Rebbe knew. I don't know how.

I was in close contact with Yeh for years. Several years later, I'll never forget, I was at another magnetohydrodynamics conference, I think it was in Pittsburgh. Usually they have a banquet, preceded by a reception. I went to the reception to see people, and then, before they went to the tables, I started to go away, because I had nothing to do there. Suddenly I heard this Yeh shouting, "Professor Branover, why are you leaving?" I said, "I'm eating kosher, so I can't stay for the meal." He said, "Of course! I took care of it! We ordered it from the airlines. Come!"

CD   *In that Yechidus and others, did the Rebbe give you an approach to the reconciliation of science and Torah?*

HB   Quite a lot. That was one of the main topics each time. I wrote a book a few years ago about some of the things I learned. It is called *Mah Rabu Maasecho*, it is written in Hebrew.

The Rebbe is the only one who makes the unequivocal statement that the many assertions in the Tanach regarding the structure of the world have to be taken literally. If the Torah says that the Earth is standing still and the sun is going around it, then it is true, even though any first grader in any school will tell you the opposite. The Rebbe is stressing the point that maybe 100 years ago, in the time of classical science, there were questions, but now, in the era of modern science, Einstein, Niels Bohr, Heisenberg, things have changed completely. This in turn is an additional proof that we are in Moshiach's era, because even the world, the material world, is ready for Moshiach. Even something which is derived from the material world, which is science, cold and detached science, is also converging back to Torah. The exact opposite of what used to be 100 years ago.

One of the examples is the structure of the world. In 1973-74 when I had just come out of Russia, Dr. Tzvi Feier, who used to be the secretary of the Organization of American Orthodox Jewish Scientists, a physicist himself, was the publisher of their magazine,

Intercom. He wrote a letter to the Rebbe, asking many questions with respect to the reconciliation of Torah and science.

He got a very detailed answer, and two or three days later the Rebbe wrote him another additional letter. Tzvi was very pleased, and he gave me the Rebbe's answers to read. He asked the Rebbe for permission to publish this in *Intercom*, which the Rebbe gave. Tzvi published it. The entire paragraph, that there was no scientific problem with the earth standing still, was not in the printed version. I called him up and asked him. He told me he was very uncomfortable including it. He said, "I think I did a good service to the Rebbe not to publish it."

I said, "Tzvi, you shouldn't have done that. The Rebbe gave you permission to publish it. The Rebbe put it in the letter for the purpose that everyone should read it!"

"Yes, but you know, that would cause all kinds of unpleasant comments, and I appreciate the Rebbe too much to involve him in this."

"Don't you think the Rebbe knows better? How do you dare to interfere?"

We organized some seminars in Crown Heights for people whose education was in physics. Some of them could learn [Torah, including chasidus] well also. Each session was a few hours. We were digging and digging, and we couldn't find where is the real proof. At Yechidus I told the Rebbe we had difficulties. He said, "You are going too far and too deep. It is on the surface. Look on the surface of Einstein's Theory of Relativity."

Still we couldn't understand. A few days later we found, in Barnes and Noble's bookstore, a book first published in 1926 by one of Einstein's closest disciples, Hans Reichenbach. This was the English translation. The title was "The Philosophy of Time and Space." He analyzes there, on a very popular level, the whole question, and shows that the heliocentric and geocentric hypotheses are equally acceptable, and that as long as Einstein's theory is accepted, science will never be able to decide between them. If both versions are acceptable, and Chumash, Gemorah, and Rambam choose one of them, why jump to the other?

Let me explain a little more. According to Einstein's theory, there is no absolute space and no absolute movement. All science can do is establish the relative velocity between two bodies. It can never say which one is moving and which one is standing still. It can never say which is on the center and which is on the periphery. That is not in the details. That is the basic concept on which the Torah is built. When we made ourselves crazy analyzing equations and more equations, it didn't help, because we went too deep.

As far as evolution and Darwin, the Rebbe shows the weakness of extrapolation, that it is not really science, just speculation which can produce any results one wants.

One area which nobody except the Rebbe has brought up, more important than all of the others from a philosophical point of view, is quantum physics. There the Rebbe always stresses the uncertainty principle, which is the opposite of all the classical science which came before. The nineteenth century science stressed that the world is deterministic, with a chain of causes and effects, and that knowing the history of a system makes it possible to completely know the present state. That whole system contradicted the basis of Yiddishkeit, which is based on free will.

According to the classical approach, Laplace wrote 200 years ago that, given the position and condition of every atom, everything could be calculated, including human behavior. For him a human being is only a machine, that obeys the laws of chemistry and physics.

The Rebbe points out that today, with Heisenberg's principle of uncertainty and the laws of quantum physics, there is no more determinism. There is a very profound parallelism between Torah and the conclusions of quantum physics. Particularly, according to quantum physics, the material universe can only exist if there is a man who perceives it. Physicists, knowing nothing about Torah, in particular the Nobelist Eugene Wigner, who was Jewish but knew nothing about Judaism, concluded that only a human being with free will could perform the function of observing a physical object. Otherwise it disappears, and becomes an assemblage of waves of probability.

There are articles in the scientific literature like this. For example, "Physics Today" in April 1985 published a big article, "Is the moon there when nobody looks." The author, by the way, was the head of the theoretical physics department of Cornell University. The answer is no — if nobody looks, scientifically, the world is not there.

Of course, we know otherwise, because the Torah tells us, "In the beginning the Lord created the heavens and the earth." But scientifically, based on perception and logic, it shouldn't exist. It comes into existence because there is a man possessing free will. Why free will? Wigner explains that free will is the only entity which is not subordinate to the laws of nature. To bring nature into existence, you need something which is higher than nature.

The Rebbe says, "Look at the parallelism with Chazal [the Jewish sages] ." In the Talmud, not just the new moon, but many, many things are established by the testimony of two witnesses. The Rebbe stresses in many of his Sichos, it is not that the testimony is derived from nature, merely a function of natural occurrences.. The moment the testimony is accepted by the Jewish court, it governs nature, not the other way around. The Torah is not derived from the world, the world is derived from Torah.

CD   *Have you tried propounding Reichenbach's explanation? Is it accepted by authentic scientists today?*

HB   I tried it on many physicists. It's a mixed reaction. First they say no, because that's the ideology they've been brought up in. When you ask them to go back to the theory [of relativity] in which they have been educated for most of their lives, and to take in account this and that, they say, "Yes, the principle is true, but we're used to so and so." That just shows that even a professional in relativity is indoctrinated by things he learned before he became a specialist. If you push them to think it through, there is no way they cannot accept it.

CD   *Have you published this? Also, did the Rebbe actually get into the scientific details of your work?*

HB   In scientific journals there is nothing to publish. I can't publish something that was said by scientists 60 years ago, because it is elementary. The real novelty is from the Torah point of view, to demonstrate, as the Rebbe did, that science is converging back to Torah.

I could give you an example in practical science. Not philosophy, but the work I have been active in.

Around 1980 we invented in my laboratory a new method for generating electricity, cheaper and cleaner environmentally. We registered patents, and I made presentations at many universities. I made a small model and demonstrated it and everyone was happy.

Then, at Yechidus, the Rebbe asked me about it. I gave him a brief answer, and the Rebbe smiled and said, "No, no. I want the presentation as you give it at universities." I felt very uncomfortable. To stand in front of the Rebbe and speak of turbulence, of magnetic fields, equations... it's irrelevant. Of course there was no blackboard and chalk, so I had to just say the equations, I couldn't write them, but everything else was the same. I tried to shorten it, but it still took at least 20 minutes.

When I finished, the Rebbe said two things. First, he told me that the method could be improved even more if certain things were changed in the mode of preparation. Nobody, not myself, my assistants, or my audiences, very distinguished people, had caught this point.

Secondly, the Rebbe said that two numbers, the system efficiency, and the two-phase flow velocity, were not compatible with each other. The Rebbe said, "You are the expert — I must believe you. But by me, these two numbers don't go together."

I didn't know what to say. I explained how we got those two numbers, the theory, the calculation, but the Rebbe insisted. I went home and I asked my assistants to check all the calculations. It was exhausting, just one of the intermediate results took 15 minutes of mainframe computer time. Finally we found the mistake. I had a new doctoral student, who had to make himself familiar with all the work which had been done. One morning he came to me and said he had difficulty understanding something. In the process of clarifying, we found that one term in a certain equation was written erroneously. When it was corrected we got completely different results.

Everyone asks me, "How did the Rebbe know?" The Rebbe didn't have a computer, that's for sure. The Rebbe didn't even use a pencil and paper. In a second, he knew.

CD   *Did these two numbers make a difference in the practical application?*

HB   Absolutely yes. All we did in those two years wasn't correct. That's in the field of pure applied science.

The greatest thing which I was privileged to hear was the prophecy about Russia, which goes back to April 1985, one week after Gorbachev took office in Moscow as General Secretary of the Communist Party, and later President.

I was at that time on Sabbatical, teaching at New York University here in Manhattan. Suddenly I got a call that the Rebbe wanted to see me. He spoke to me at the door of his room. It was a short Yechidus, a few minutes. The Rebbe told me I should try to reach by phone all of my contacts in Moscow, Leningrad and other cities, and tell them that they should be assured that from now on the situation in Russia will improve. Not immediately, it will take time, but that the whole thing will fall apart and communism will come to an end, and that whoever wishes to leave will be allowed, and anyone who wishes to stay will be able to practice Yiddishkeit.

For me it was wonderful. I was full of joy, even though I couldn't see how this could come. In our conception, Communist Russia was eternal. No power in the world could destroy it, but the Rebbe is the Rebbe.

On the way back, I stopped to buy the papers. The New York Times had headlines proclaiming that the new leader in the Kremlin will be worse than the previous ones, and these will be difficult times, the Post likewise. OK, all the experts are on one side and the Rebbe is on the other side. At that time it didn't surprise me already. I had plenty of experience. I went to make the calls. I spent two days, it was very difficult at that time to get through, but I contacted maybe a dozen people. They were very encouraged, but at the same time they felt skepticism. One told me that his wife had been taken to the KGB for interrogation three days before and had not come home yet. A second told me that a KGB car is standing at his door day and night — "If the Rebbe says so, it's wonderful, but we don't see it. It's getting worse."

I wrote a note to the Rebbe. I got an answer, "Yes, it can't be seen yet, but the process is already on its way." He instructed me to call them again and reassure them again. I did this, and everyone knows what happened later. All the so-called Sovietologists were absolutely wrong. It collapsed.

The end of the story is that three years ago, which is seven years after this instruction I got, Gorbachev visited Israel. One day he was a guest of our university, and, as I speak Russian, they asked me to be in charge of his reception and so on. I used the opportunity to tell Gorbachev and his wife about this great leader, this great Tzaddik in NY who told me all this.

Gorbachev told me it was impossible. I told him, "How can you say that to me? I have the first-hand information."

He said, "I will explain. In April 1985 I didn't have the slightest idea what I was going to do. I had no plan." He told me that even though he knew about the Chabadniks, and it was possible they could have penetrated his office, it wouldn't have helped, because there were no papers and no conversations to spy on, simply because there were no ideas. A year or two later, he had a plan, but he never implemented it. The changes in Russia were leading to the exact opposite of what he wanted. He wanted an improved version of communism, which no one accepted.

To me, this is not a forecast, not a prediction. It is Nevuah, real prophecy. This is something that could not have been figured out rationally, because it was not in anyone's head. This the Rebbe predicted precisely.

This was prophecy of a global scale. It influenced not just Russian Jews, or Russians in general. It changed the whole world.

CD   *From 1973 to 1985, did you and the Rebbe correspond regarding Russian Jewry?*

HB   Very much. First, the Rebbe instructed us to revive Jewish culture in the Russian language. We founded Shamir [publishing], which has by now published over 50 books, a huge library, with more than 5 million copies published. They are distributed mostly in Russia, but also in America and Israel. The Rebbe went into the tiniest details. We had questions of translation, the language to use, editing. The modern Russian language, after 70 years of Communism, didn't have words relevant to spiritual concepts. You could hardly say "G-d", "miracle", "spirit". If you did it sounded so old-fashioned it gave an erroneous conception. The Rebbe, mainly orally in Yechidus, went into a whole investigation of how to do this.

When we translated the very first book, we sent a copy to the Rebbe. I was shocked. The Rebbe did a full editing and proof-reading job in Russian. It's unbelievable. On every page, and many times, more than once on a page, corrections in grammar, spelling. I cannot imagine the Rebbe sitting and doing this. It was a big book of several hundred pages typewritten. We got it out with all the corrections.

Later we always got advice on what to publish, how to distribute to books in Russia, approaches in editorial philosophy and halachic points. The tiniest, tiniest details. When we started to translate the Chumash, how to translate the various names of G-d, Hava'ye and Elokim. We did this completely different from the way others are doing it, because the Rebbe's approach was completely different. This was so that the Russians who read it would perceive everything properly.

CD   *Can you please give an example?*

HB   I'll have to use Russian words. For example, for Elokim, the Rebbe gave a whole explanation that this name indicates forcefulness, and therefore we have to use the Russian word "Disilne", about equivalent to "The most powerful". It was never used in theological literature in Russian, but in our Chumash we use this term.

The Rebbe told us that most of the publications, including chasidus and the Rebbe's Sichos, have to be translated in what he called a "journalistic modern language, a newspaper language" so that it would be easy to read. The exception would be the Chumash and the Siddur, where the language should be a little archaic, so people should perceive that this is a special book.

Then of course, there were instructions on the more physical aspects, how to help bring people closer to Yiddishkeit, how to deal with the education of children. The Rebbe said the first step is to deal with the physical side of things, to become a good friend, help them in material things.

Then, when we started sending Shluchim in to Russia, years before Gorbachev, there were similar instructions on what to do and what not to do. Such a person in those years was not only endangering himself, he was putting in danger those who might visit him, and the Rebbe told us how to overcome these problems.

We spoke before about elevated philosophy, and miracles. Sometimes the Rebbe acts on the level of the spiritual authority, but sometimes he is acting on the level of a real manager, a practical manager. An unbelievable combination.

CD   *I heard that the Rebbe was not so much in support of the Soviet Jewry demonstrations in the 70's. Did you discuss this?*

HB   Yes, many times. The Rebbe explained that the harm of noisy demonstrations is not only that it could anger the Soviet authorities. He wanted to maintain peace with the Soviet authorities because so many Jews were living there, totally dependent on them.

This is no contradiction to his pointing out that under the Soviet constitution the Jews are allowed to study the Torah and teach their children and so on, and that in speaking to a policeman one should take out a copy of the Russian constitution and show him that it allows freedom of religion. The Rebbe wanted to be firm and strong, but merely to anger the authorities was counterproductive.

He also explained more than once that this is not the only reason, or even the main reason, why he is opposed to demonstrations. He told me once, in Yechidus, that when you have a huge rally here in New York, a quarter of a million people, they go out on a nice Sunday morning, good weather, they take a walk, they feel very good about themselves, and then they go home and feel they did their best.

It's bad enough that this demonstrations did more harm than good. It's even more harmful that this person went home with the feeling that he did his best and contributed. If, after this, you will approach this person and ask him for a hundred dollars to send a parcel to Russia with clothes which [when sold] will sustain a family for a month or two, he will say, "Go to someone else. I already demonstrated." This happened! I myself had the experience many times.

We see that ultimately it was Hashem who helped, not the demonstrations, or the call for demonstrations. In retrospect it looks silly. Jews came out in masses not because of any demonstrations, but because the Soviet Union fell apart.

CD   *Did the Rebbe have any contact with officials of the Russian government in those years?*

HB   Maybe, but nothing I know of.

CD   *There was a Lag B'Omer parade in the Eighties when the Rebbe began to speak in Russian. At that time he also spoke about the Russian Constitution. Was there any event at the time that may have sparked this?*

HB   The Rebbe wanted to say two things. First, to explain to Russian Jews that without Torah, Jewish life is not a life, and that they had to give some Torah knowledge to their children. Secondly, he wanted to encourage them, and let them know that according to the Constitution they are permitted. The inertia of being scared outlasted Stalin for several decades. Under Stalin, what could you do, but under Brezhnev people could do it, they just didn't dare to do it. The Rebbe told them not to be scared, take the Constitution, speak to the policeman, speak to the clerk. I know some people who did do it and, Boruch Hashem, nothing happened to them.

CD   **In other words, they were allowed to do it under Brezhnev's** *rule.*

HB   Yes. When I was in Russia most of the people wouldn't even dare do something toward the education of their children. Some religious people sent their children to the public schools. They didn't want to fight, they even sent children to school on Shabbos. A very few others spoke openly and boldly to the principal of the school, "We are religious. Our religion does not permit the child to go to Shabbos, and I will not send him. I am not going to make excuses and pretexts."

I know examples where it worked. The only problem is that school starts on September 1. There is one Shabbos and then another where the child does not show up at school, and suddenly he disappears for several days. The principal gets angry and calls the father, "what happened now. It's not Saturday?" He says, "Now it's Rosh Hashanah and Sukkos..."

CD   *What happened in 1987 when the Rebbe said a special sicha for you and Rabbi Shlomo Madanchik?*

HB   This was two years after he had predicted, with his prophetic vision, that change was on the way, but it was well before the mass emigration. There had been a few changes, but the mass emigration began in 1989. The Rebbe said a very special Sichah, Shabbos Hagodol. He mentioned that there were certain subjects which he did not want to discuss on Shabbos, and there would be another Farbrengen Motzoei Shabbos. Then he spoke of the necessity to build a Chabad town in Jerusalem, with a Jewish style, and a Jewish approach. He made hints that it was for Russian Jews, who would begin coming in greater numbers. He developed this quite at length.

After the Farbrengen, Shlomo Madanchik and I got a call from the Rebbe's Secretariat, saying we should come for Yechidus. The Rebbe gave us details. In the Sichah he had spoken in general terms, without giving technicalities. In the Yechidus he told us that we should go to certain Government ministers, to the Prime Minister, and explain these details. The Rebbe also told us that there is an argument in Israel about the phenomenon of those Jews who come out of the Soviet Union, and drop out of Aliyah in Rome, to go to the United States or other countries.

The Rebbe said that his advice to every Soviet Jew who is already on his way is that he should go to Israel and never leave Israel. The Rebbe asked to publicize this. He stressed that this project is a kind of a pilot project. It should be done very fast. It should be large, but it is much more important to have it ready within half a year. The minimum was to build fifty houses. Also, employment was a necessity. Since the majority of Soviet Jews are scientists and engineers, it is necessary to provide them with work in their profession.

It looked impossible in practical terms. To build in Eretz Yisroel, or anywhere else for that matter, takes at least a year from the start, plans, permits. We had more meetings, because the government wanted to give us space outside Jerusalem, and the Rebbe wanted it to be inside the borders of Jerusalem.

I came from several meetings with city officials, the Ministry of Housing, and others, and I brought maps of Jerusalem to show him the places they offered us. I took out the maps. I remember the detail the Rebbe brought in discussing the neighborhoods. This place, if the husband has to go to a convention in Binyanei HaUmah, it will take him so much time, and if the housewife wants to go shopping in the city center she will have to pass such and such streets. I am in Jerusalem two or three times a week and I have no idea of most of those streets, and everyone knows the Rebbe never was in Yerushalayim.

The time factor looked impossible, but we find a block of 52 houses which had almost been finished by a contractor. We purchased them, and established the SATEC industrial company which today employs more than a hundred immigrants from Russia.

Unfortunately, we could not go beyond this. The Rebbe had told us to give an example, and that we did fulfill. Nobody in Israel, the Minister of Housing, of Absorption, at that time they did not speak of immigration, and here, suddenly, Chabad is building a whole neighborhood, a small one but a neighborhood, especially for Russian Jews, with employment. Suddenly all these officials were running around, looking for more builders. The Rebbe's encouragement reached all.

We were able to appreciate what the Rebbe had said, that small but fast was better than large and slow. It became an issue all over Israel.

Then we wanted to build a second, much larger building, and we got into endless bureaucratic problems. Ultimately they passed a law which denies giving any areas to private initiatives to build neighborhoods. That was years later.

The big thing is that it made a big impact on the whole mood and attitude of the people concerned with immigration, to alert them that a large immigration was to come and what they had to do for it.

Ultimately, I was nominated by Yitzchok Shamir to the Prime Minister's commission on the employment of immigrants, of where I am to this day.

CD   *What exactly is SATEC?*

HB   Shamir Advanced Technology Engineering Center. Now we also have ONT, which is Olim Negev Technology.

CD   *Do you have plans for the future?*

HB   The whole idea at the beginning was that it's only a prototype. More were supposed to come. On the other hand, I don't think that the Rebbe intended for it to be an absorption center for the whole 600,000 Jews who were going to come. As Madanchik and I understand, I think we fulfilled the Rebbe's conception. We reported positively, but he never pushed for more, so I assume that the idea was to provide an impetus and set a certain standard to be copied.

As a matter of fact, our industries together employ about 130 people. A drop in the sea. But it created a model, and the plan which we presented to the Prime Minister for absorbing all the Russian Jews became totally accepted by the experts as the solution. They figured that if Israel could establish 500 industries like that, it would take car of all the population of immigrants.

CD   *What is your opinion of the current situation of these 600,000 immigrants?*

HB   Nowadays the situation is very tough regarding the immigration scene. This is an anti-Jewish government. It doesn't care about the Jews, just wants to be nice to the Arabs and get all kinds of international awards. They don't care whatsoever. You cannot move them. It seems absolutely hopeless, and that's one of the tragedies. Immigration started on its high level in 1989. 200,000 people in one year. The subsequent year also, then it started going down and down. Now it's at its lowest, not only in numbers, but in quality, who is coming. Younger people stopped coming, now we are getting only pensioners. This is also good, they are also Jews, but for the economy of the country it's a burden.

People with ten, twenty, thirty years left in their working lives, have stopped coming. I get statistics from reliable sources. From 1989 till now Israel got 60,000 engineers. Before the immigration Israel had 29,000 engineers. It tripled the number of engineers, and it doubled the number of scientists.

Out of the 60,000 engineers, only 12,000 are working in anything close to their profession. All the rest are either getting subsidies, or they are sweeping streets and washing dishes and wasting completely their talents. They brought in to the country more than 100,000 patents, inventions, projects, because in Russia the government encourages this. They pour in money, endless, billions and trillions. These people are bringing these things and asking to use them. Nobody cares.

CD   *What about your programs in Russia, are you able to continue printing books and disseminating Judaism?*

HB   Of course we continue. Books in great number, all kinds of books. Fundamental material like Chumashim with commentaries, Shulchan Aruch, Siddur, Rambam. Also books about Yiddishkeit like Herman Wouk's *The Synagogue,* Chaim Donin's *To Be a Jew,*

A Jew in his Home by Kitov. Also books for youth, some fiction if it has a Jewish content.

We are running two day schools, a tremendous burden but also a tremendous accomplishment. Our school, which is recognized by the government, is a real Jewish Day School, up-to-date. In Riga there is a governmental school which is called "The Jewish School", but it's secular. We reached an agreement with the government that we would provide Jewish teachers for all grades, 1 to 11 — there are 11 grades in Russia. We teach Jewish history, tradition, holidays and so on. We also provide kosher lunches in both schools, for all 800 kids.

A new project is an encyclopedia of Russian Jewry, which was initiated with the permission of the Russian government and the Russian Academy of Sciences. It is amazing how much it changed. Something for which one could have been shot or sent to Siberia for life! Instead, the government has asked me, knowing that we are the biggest publisher of Jewish books in the Russian language, to become the editor in chief. This will be a seven-volume work.

In another project in Moscow, about 200 historians and scholars are researching the archives that were opened up, from the KGB, the Communist party, etc. They are very nice to me. I was thrown out as a traitor, now they beg me to agree to be elected to the Academy.

CD   *Are they financing all the 200 people?*

HB   Not the whole thing. With money they are always not very good. But they participate. They gave us the permission, they opened the archives, and they gave some money, but most of the money still has to be raised.

CD   *I've heard a story many times about you and the Rebbe concerning solar energy.*

HB   That was the story I told you. The invention had to do with electric power, it had a broader scope, but at that time the main

24

interest was to generate electricity from solar heat. Maybe I didn't mention that. Because, looking retrospectively, it's not just for solar, it's for any source of heat.

CD   *Did the Rebbe speak to you about personal issues, family issues? Did he give you guidance in your personal Yiddishkeit also, as an individual, not just science?*

HB   Of course! Every time. He gave Brochos and advice. Also, in our discussions on Torah and Science, at certain moments he would stop himself and say with a smile, "Don't think that I am so interested in your science! For me it's important that through your science one more Jew will put on Tefillin." That happened several times. Mainly it was through discussing the Torah books in the Russian language, of which in many cases I was the editor. Inevitably it went into all sorts of Jewish issues, how to understand the basics of the Torah and Rambam etc.

CD   *Tell us a little about your feelings toward the Rebbe. How do you see him as a global leader?*

HB   I perceive the Rebbe as alive. I just have to make an effort to stay close with him, and I believe that depends on the individual, on his faith and conviction. That is what he has to accomplish.

    I always say that when I and others reach a degree of confidence which will be equal to our degree of confidence in the coming of Moshiach, for instance in the fact that tomorrow morning the sun will rise then he will be here already. Actually here we should have greater confidence, because the rising of the sun is an empirical fact. The Rebbe always stresses that a Jew puts seeds in the ground not because of empirical evidence, but because he believes in G-d.

    I believe in the sun rising because experience teaches us. As far as the coming of Moshiach we have the words of the Rebbe himself, when he spoke of prophecy, when he spoke of the seventh generation, going back to the demand of the Baal Shem Tov to spread out the wellsprings of Chasidus, and no one, in all the generations, spread them out more than the Rebbe.

No question it's difficult, because we still stick to our rational thinking, and we are surrounded by this world, especially now, with computers and airplanes. There is a tendency to believe in what we see and experience, and not what we should take into consideration.

CD   *Is there a scientific analogy to something existing on the spiritual and physical planes at the same time?*

HB   In this science is converging to Torah. I could suggest those things I just spoke about to scientists, which are very symptomatic. Just a few months ago, two remarkable books were published. One was in Moscow University, formerly a hotbed of atheism, by professor Yuri Vladimirov, *Fundamental Physics of Religion*. Of course he's a Christian, it's not for us, but according to their approaches he shows the validity of religion in view of modern fundamental physics.

More interesting is a book by Frank Tippler, an American physicist, published in America by Doubleday, called Physics of Immortality. The subtitle is "Modern Cosmology, G-d, and Resurrection of the Dead". It's about 700 pages, about 200 pages of pure mathematics, equations and so on. In his conclusions, which include the Deity, resurrection of the Dead, Divine Providence, Free Will, he writes that he came to them not by religion, he used to be a confirmed atheist, but just through analyzing laws of physics and so on. He speaks not only of scientific possibility of Resurrection of the Dead, but inevitability.

You ask me how the two can be reconciled. The mere appearance of these books shows something. No publishing house, ten years ago, even five years ago would dare to publish such a book. No physicist would dare to write it, because they would be ostracized by the other physicists. Nowadays the world is already different. I'm not saying there are no exceptions, but the general outlook Is different.

Going back to your question, even science, which is so cold and rational, so distant from us, is coming to the same conclusions.

2

Mr. Herb Brin

Publisher, Editor (Heritage group of Jewish
newspapers in California), Poet, Author

FIGHTING JOURNALIST

CD   *I'd like to begin by asking you where and when you were
born and how you got started as a journalist.*

HB   It's a long story but I'll tell it briefly. My name is Herb Brin.
Last February 17th I observed my 80th birthday, and I'll be bar
mitzvah again in three years! (His 83rd birthday) Nothing will stop
me. I'd like that to be understood. I came through the battles in the
early part of the century, the Jews and the Polocks in Chicago.
Everywhere I'd go they were yelling "zhid" at Jews. I didn't take
too kindly to this, and I would fight morning, noon and night with
the "bums" who dared to attack our people. This was on Carmott
Avenue on the Northwest side of Chicago. I come from an orthodox, strictly orthodox Jewish family. My uncle was trustee and
president of the Crystal Street Shul, one of the most respected
orthodox people in the city. We had a strictly kosher home, but
when it came to my going to cheder to learn Yiddishkeit and to
learn to davenn, I was so busy fighting the Polacken kids that I was
kicked out of cheder.

CD   *You literally fought with them?*

HB   I fought with them physically. There was no chochmas
about it. My mother used to say, "doh vakst a bum [a bum is grow-

27

ing up here]". She meant it literally.

HB   My mother was from Minskya Gobernya, Pyotrkov. My father was from Poland, from Ponin. My father's family was half Sefardic and half Ashkenazic, and comes from a very prominent German Jewish family, including Maximilian Hardin, who was a press attaché for Bismarck. That was my father's first cousin. Another first cousin was Henry Gussenstein, who was the great sculptor of Israel and won the Prix de Rome twice. He was a very gifted sculptor.

How it happened that I got into poetry, I don't know, but this is my special art field. I still can't davenn. I know a lot of the prayers by rote. I can go into a shul and people will think that I am davenning, but I'm not. I know what the prayers are through long memories.

I became a newsman in Chicago. In Los Angeles I was a feature writer for the LA times from 1946 to 1954. In 1954, I left the LA Times because I felt guilty that I didn't do enough to fight the Germans. Although, in 1938-39 I joined the Anti-Defamation League as a spy. I'm six foot one, I have blue eyes and perfectly blonde hair, and they entered me as a Nazi. I joined the Nazi Party in Chicago, and the ADL knew every single move that the Nazi Party was planning.

There were a few others, we knew all the parades with the swastikas and the whole thing. We had Jewish guys organized, and we beat them up at the parades. I'll tell you, it wasn't healthy to be a Nazi in Chicago.

CD   *You infiltrated them.*

HB   I infiltrated them, and this has been my work all my life. That's why I left the LA Times. I felt I didn't do enough to fight Hitler in Germany. I was on limited service because of a training accident. My legs had been broken. I was offered a medical discharge but I refused to take it. I stayed on. I interviewed all the top generals for all the top newspapers. The New York Times, The Washington Post, LA Times, Christian Science Monitor, Dallas

Morning News, all of the top daily newspapers in the US. Stillwell, General Grove who directed the Manhattan Project.

I felt that I didn't do enough. I didn't do enough.

I left the Los Angeles Times. I was their top feature writer. I started a little Jewish newspaper. Who is crazy enough to start a Jewish newspaper? I came to New York and met with some friends of mine. One was Charlie Roth, who was a friend of Lubavitch.

The other one was Gabe Cohen of the Jewish Post and Opinion of Indianapolis. He's still publishing, right now. Charlie Roth said. "I want to take you two to the Lubavitcher Rebbe." This was me and Gabe Cohen. I said fine. He said "We'll meet at midnight. It'll take a minute or two and then we'll leave. We'll have some late supper and then we'll go." This happened in 1954.

CD   *You had never heard of the Lubavitcher Rebbe?*

HB   I had heard of the Lubavitcher Rebbe, but not that much. I had just started the Heritage. Why not do the right thing?

I was taken down by Charlie Roth and Gabe Cohen. They sat outside. They figured I would go in for one minute. The Rebbe would shmeichel [glad-hand] at me a little bit and let me go, and then they would go in. They're sitting there, and the guy with the beady eyes was out there. He looked through me, and he said, "OK, you go in first."

The Rebbe got up and welcomed me. I was so delighted to see that the Rebbe spoke English and I wouldn't have to use my broken Yiddish — I was terrified there might be no communication — What am I going in for, to waste his time?

CD   *Your parents spoke Yiddish?*

HB   At home. I learned English when I was six. We were Yiddishists.

The Rebbe greeted me in English. He told me a little bit first about his own background. He knew my background, that I was at the LA times, that I was a leading journalist. Certainly in the metropolitan field I was well known.

We started talking, telling me about his going to the Sorbonne, getting a degree in engineering. He mentioned other universities too. He looked pretty much like you have him now, a little thinner. It was an austere room. I remember the wood, it was oak flooring. Everything was wood. I don't remember there being a carpet in that room. Austere but very, very relaxing. You knew that this was a man who used the books, and was highly intellectual in this field.

Suddenly he looks at me, and says, "I know you have a question to ask."

I said, "Yes I do. I've got to ask you, who are a leader in our community, do I have a right to act as an editor and write editorials for a Jewish newspaper, when I know so little of Yiddishkeit, when I can't even davenn." I just put it on the line, "What right do I have to serve as the editor of a Jewish newspaper? Maybe I'm in the wrong field after all?"

We talked about education, he brought the story about the child who whistled in the balcony, and the Rebbe said that's also his form of prayer.

I said "Rabbi, I don't whistle in balconies. I've got to know that I'm doing the right thing." He smiled. Apparently he enjoyed talking with me, as I suddenly enjoyed talking with him. It was a mutual respect.

CD   *You told him simply, you need to know right here?*

HB   I told him my background, fighting for Jewish causes physically, and how I was kicked out of cheder, I can't davenn, my Bar Mitzvah was a fake. Not a fake entirely. My father wrote out in English a transliteration of the parsha, the Haftorah, the blessings. I memorized it and that was my Bar Mitzvah. They even gave me a gold star. The gave you a gold star if you did exceptionally well. Besides being a fighter, I had a background of reading a great deal. I read all the classics.

Then the Rebbe did a startling thing. He got up from his chair, at the desk. I was sitting there, so I got up too. Was this the end of the interview? Then, by the way, this was already fifteen or twenty minutes. I was thinking about these guys in the hallway. They just said it would take me a minute or two, and I felt embarrassed. I was going to bow out or something.

He got up and reached in to his wallet. "How much is a subscription to your newspaper?"

I said, "Three dollars and fifty cents."

He took out three dollars, and gave me fifty cents in cash, "I want a subscription."

He had a subscription. I am near tears now, as I'm telling this. He had a subscription for the rest of his life to Heritage. He said something, the most significant thing he's ever said to me. He looked at me right square in the eye and he said , "Do you have a right to withhold that which you know? Obviously you're a learned man. You've read a great deal. Do you have a right to withhold that which you know?"

I took the money and I remained editor of a Jewish newspaper.

He directed me in this path. Could I not support the Lubavitch movement? I would be an ingrate. And I've never failed the Lubavitch movement.

CD   *As far as your Yechidus?*

HB   He said, we cannot turn our back on the young Jewish people there are today. We must embrace them. He's looking at me and I can tell he's embracing me in the process. I'm part of the thing. We had a long discussion on this, on the rights of Jews to maintain Judaism in our time, the time of Hitler, or the time of after Hitler, because this was just after Hitler, just after the holocaust, a disastrous time for us.

He knew why I was in Jewish journalism, because of my not having fought hard enough against the Nazis. I started telling him some of the problems I'm facing as a Jewish editor. I said, "I'm having a problem with the fact that a number of our Jewish leaders, including David Ben-Gurion, are racing to embrace the Germans, for money." The week before, Israel had announced it was going to take up the sale of Israeli arms to Germany.

I asked the Rebbe the question, "Does Israel, does Ben Gurion, have the right to sell arms to Germany, the destroyer of our people?"

He said, "Absolutely not!"

I asked him if I could quote him. He said, "Yes, you may."

He gave me a long [newspaper] story on the obligation leadership has not to forget the victims of the Fuehrer. That's how I wrote the story. It was a sensational story. Other newspapers around the country picked it up. It was my paper. He gave me the story and I wrote it. That's my role as a journalist.

He gave me the right to do this, to write about his point of view on Ben Gurion and selling arms to Germany.

The following week, it appeared in the New York Times, all the major newspapers — if they didn't quote my story in my name, they said it in the Rebbe's name. They checked with the Rebbe's secretaries and confirmed it, because, after all, it was the truth. He had given me the authority to do it, and I did it.

Anyway, this is one of the elements that came up, but the big thing that he told me to watch out for was the move into the educational field of the Lubavitcher movement. This I had also known, long before you got to know it on the scale that it happened later.

CD   *Could you be more specific?*

HB   He said, "We have another role to play, and that's to bring Yiddishkeit, Jewishness, to Jews. It will be on a major level throughout the world." And he did!

CD   *He was telling you about his plans?*

HB   Not the specific plans, but the general outlines. I said to him, "You're a young man" — he was a young man — "you must have plans — what are your plans for the Jewish people?" I asked him whether he was going to go to Israel at any time, and he avoided me, he didn't answer the question. I guess it was within him, and he was thinking it over.

Not that he avoided me, but that it was a question that he had to confront.

CD   *Did you ask him about how he became a Rebbe?*

HB   No. There are things that I didn't ask him that I would ask him now. Old Charlie Roth took me in for one minute. I had no plan, no idea for six hours of discussion. Do you know this discussion that I've abbreviated here took six hours. As the sky became bright he got up and we walked out together, side-by-side, arm in arm. He turned to the left going towards his home and I turned to the right going towards the train station back to Manhattan.

CD   *Who did most of the talking?*

HB   He did. I did a lot of talking too, because of my role in coming back to Yiddishkeit, to Jewishness. I assured him I would never let him down, which I never did. We're sitting in the shul right now, and I never let him down, never once!

CD   *In the years following 1954, did you ever again have a meeting with the Rebbe?*

HB   Never did, but I wrote to him on a number of occasions, and his secretary conveyed his answers. The things that I needed were personal things, Misheberach's, health, and things like that, which I do to this day, even if he's "gone". My witness is Rabbi Raichik

CD   *Since 1954 you never saw him again in person.*

HB   Never did.

CD   *Why didn't you make another trip?*

HB   I wanted to, but I didn't. I felt I was an embarrassment to him. After all, I was a young man. I took advantage of him. I didn't feel that I had the learning. At every time in my life, if I were

33

told that I would go in to meet with the Rebbe under those kinds of conditions, I would not have done it. I don't have that, it is chutz-pah, audacity. I feel that I would be unkind, unfair to the Rebbe, the kind of a person, the kind of a background I have. I just kept my distance.

CD   *Looking back 40 years, as a poet and a writer, someone who's gone through so much — what do you say about him?*

HB   I think his imprint on our people, our community, will be remembered 500 years from now the way we remember the Rambam.

I would say this — by electing another Lubavitcher Rebbe you're not pre-empting his role. It just happens, an accident of Jewish life, a man of this quality emerged. The same kind of person will not emerge again. It's not possible that you or you or you will become a Lubavitcher Rebbe. So don't even look at it that way. All you know is that you have a personality, a persona, who gave qualities to a movement that transcended the movement itself. When I said he would be on the level of the Rambam, I mean it. I've met with Ben Gurion many times — before and since. I've met with Abba Eban and Golda Meir, Shazar, but the experience with the Lubavitcher Rebbe stands alone — you can't compare. You have a man here who is in the 20th century completely. He was a 20th century man, living in the day of Hitler, the worst pogroms, the worst Shoah to take place in history against our people. He was the leader and he had many, many responsibilities. But he said, "We cannot turn our back on the Jewish educational processes that transcend all humanity."

CD   *Did you see the Rebbe's love for every Jew?*

HB   There was the Shechinah about him. He had the concerns of many, many people. Everyone wants his advice, and it becomes difficult for him, but with me he let loose. I asked him for nothing — He offered me $3.50!

CD   *When you heard the Rebbe passed on, what were your thoughts?*

HB   I cried. It was just a disaster of a day. Afterwards they asked me to come to San Diego. I had written a story and they asked me to come to the Chabad event there. I think they considered it the most important address.
      Read the books and you'll see. I'm a Democrat politically. These things I don't know — I don't ask questions. All I know is that when it comes to defending our people I found the Lubavitcher Rebbe a kindred spirit.

CD   *You were able to relate to him — just like you're a fighter, he's a fighter.*

HB   That's right. No question about it. That is the whole thing we're about. You'll find nobody with a deeper feeling of love and respect for one human being.

CD   *What did Charlie Roth and Gabe Cohen have to say? They didn't get a chance to go in!*

HB   Charlie waited for me, but the other guy left about one or two o'clock in the morning, and said, "The Rebbe must think you're more important than I am!"
      I didn't intend to do that. However, when you're involved in discussions involving major ideas like that, you do not look at the clock. It's amazing that he would, he could pinpoint these things one after another. He would suggest something, I would suggest something and that's the way we went. It was not a case that he expected obeisance from me. I'm not capable of doing that. He got from me the ultimate respect, one human to another. So that's it.

3

Mrs. Shoshana Cardin

Chairman United Israel Appeal, National Vice Chair United Jewish Appeal

SOVIET JEWRY

CD   *Could you begin with a brief history about yourself, how you got involved with Lubavitch, and the Lubavitcher Rebbe?*

SC   I guess you would say that I grew up in a family that was very Jewish, although not necessarily as devoted to ritual as people who consider themselves "dati", might be. My grandfather was named after the first Lubavitcher Rebbe, which I did not know until Lubavitch came to Baltimore and I met with Rabbi Kaplan. He contacted my husband, of blessed memory, and asked him if he would assist in hosting a Friends of Chabad evening. Jerry asked me how I would feel about that, since we hosted almost everyone who was into a Jewish cause or a communal cause that was valid. I said sure and we hosted the first Friends of Chabad evening in Baltimore. We became very friendly with Rabbi Kaplan and remained friends with him over the years, to this day.

I was born in Tel Aviv and raised in Baltimore. I worked with Israeli bonds beginning in 1959. I chaired the high holiday campaign in Baltimore, going from shul to shul to encourage people to buy bonds, then I became chairman of the women's division . I worked for JNF. As a matter of fact, I had started collecting for JNF when I was 10 years old, all the pushkas, going from place to place. Then I became active in the federation and UJA and became president of the women's division, then chairman of the Federation itself in Baltimore in 1984 and in between did many things for my

Shul. I sat on the youth activities board of the shul, I took care of youth services for the High Holy days. So in general, my involvement in Jewish life and Jewish community has been constant.

I've been going to Israel for years, I started going in 1960 and I've gone every year at least 2 or 3 times since then.

CD   *I know you had a big involvement in Russian Jewry in the 70's.*

SC   In the 70's, and then in the 80's . In the 70's as a volunteer but not as a leader, one of the amcha, ordinary people, so to speak, but very vocal. I went with the protests to Washington but in the 80's I was asked to chair the National Conference of Soviet Jewry. I did not chair until 88, because I was president of the Council of Jewish Federations from 1984 to 1987 which was a major responsibility, and it was then that I began to go to Jerusalem, just to speak on Chok Mi Yehudi, the whole issue of who the Israeli government is going to consider to be a Jew. First in 85, it was the national coalition government, so we went to speak to both Prime Minister Shamir and Prime Minister Peres. And they thought it was unimportant.

CD   *The coalition?*

SC   Yes, each individually and both together thought I was exaggerating the response that would take place in the United States among American Jews. And then again, this was with Prime Minister Shamir in 1986, and again we were not met with warm hands. They did not understand what I was trying to say, or, as the Prime Minister said, "Don't worry, Mrs. Cardin, you'll live with it if we pass it, you'll live with it if we don't pass it, everything will be all right." I tried to explain to him that that was not what I was sensing in the country, and this went on for two or three years. I went to the president, and to the prime ministers, and to the government, and to the members of the Knesset as well.

CD   *So your position was ...*

SC   The Knesset shouldn't change, shouldn't make any changes in the law, that was not the purview of the Knesset.

In that period I wrote to the Rebbe. Because I did research when the law was changed, and on what the Rebbe's position was based, and my information was also that there were representatives of Lubavitch in Jerusalem who were trying to get the law changed. So I wrote a letter expressing, our situation, our concern, and wanting either to meet with him or get a response from him. I received no response to that letter, but I did receive a response from Rabbi Kaplan, in Baltimore, who called and asked if he could visit. He came over and explained that the Rebbe had said at a public gathering he would not discuss this issue in public. He had written, I believe, his position paper in 1971, he felt very clear about that position, he chose not to discuss it, and he would not be responding to my letter.

CD   *I do not believe the Rebbe published a position paper. In fact the Rebbe did speak about it, very forcefully at his farbrengen's for over 13 years!*
What was your letter about?

SC   What I wanted was an opportunity to explain why I, not Shoshana Cardin the individual, but Shoshana Cardin representative of the federation movement, felt Chok Mihu Yehudi would split the Jewish world. As proved in November of 88, it was an explosion that covered the country. So we had the modern Orthodox movement, we had the reform and conservative movements of course, and we had individuals, key lay leaders in the country in various positions in various organizations, who were terribly, terribly upset. I heard this quietly, over the years, and I wanted to explain to the Rebbe that if this went ahead we would have a rupture in the relationship between American Jewry and Israel. It wasn't worth the price.

CD   *Mrs. Cardin, I want you to know that the Rebbe never changed his mind as far as the issue itself. The issue is not a*

38

Lubavitch agenda, it is a halachic, Torah issue, universal to all Jews. The Rebbe's directive to his emmisaries was not to get involved, however Torah does not change. Therefore the Rebbe words do not change because all the Rebbe was doing was echoing the Torah's position.

SC   I understand but disagree, as I mentioned earlier. Regardless, the Rebbe's directive to his emissaries didn't resolve the issue, because the issue was still alive in Israel, and what I wanted to do was to quiet it here. Obviously I did not succeed until 1988 when the election was so close that we didn't know who was the winner. When Prime Minister Shamir was able to put together his government, my concern was that both parties at that time would make a deal, and the deal was going to be on Chok Mihu Yehudi. So we had that whole storm, where I offered to go over and to meet the first of a series of delegations and made very big, and very public, and very well-known in Israel what our concern was.

I felt the average Israeli voter didn't care, and certainly didn't know, what the issue was. I helped develop the strategy, that we would have a series of delegations going to visit and would finally have an impact on the government. I believe we had some impact, I don't think we were the only ones who had an impact, that is, American Jewry, but I think we had a definite impact.

By then they realized how disturbed we were by the possible rift, and it just so happened that worldly events in addition assisted us. Arafat was behaving in a negative way, and people wanted a strong government and the government was formed without promising. But I will say that the Prime Minister assured me that he would not initiate the change in legislation. He didn't assure me of anything if someone else initiated it, but he wouldn't. And he had already appointed a committee, which he was chairing, to defuse the issue. And as you know, until this day, nothing has really happened even though the issue has come up again.

Rabbi Kaplan invited me to go and meet the Rebbe. And of course I accepted the invitation and I went up there. It was a public dinner, I mean that there were other lay leaders who were invited there, but I was told that I would have 3-5 minutes to speak to the

Rebbe. Even though I felt he was briefed by the Shluchim, obviously, because he had all these people, he had to know who they are, I was impressed by the fact that he chose to say , "I know I owe you a letter," which was very impressive. I mean, I'm sure Rabbi Kaplan told him, but the fact is he chose to say that.

CD   *I don't think Rabbi Kaplan told him.*

SC   Even if he didn't, the fact that he chose to acknowledge that I wrote to him on a subject which he didn't want to discuss, meant that he knew where I was, and I thought, that, was very telling. That was literally the opening sentence of our meeting, and then he asked me a few things about what I was doing with Soviet Jewry and encouraged me; He said, "You have a great deal of work to do. You are doing a very good job and you must continue We have to do everything we can , it's very important. "What you are doing is good, it's holy work, and be strong and continue." Then we discussed a few other issues about Soviet Jewry, because that was the beginning of Soviet Jews being able to come to the United States, which there hadn't legitimately been before, and going to Israel. He encouraged me to work for them in going to Israel, and to keep up my strength, and that I was doing good things for the Jewish people.

CD   *He encouraged them to go to Israel rather than the United States? Is that the point?*

SC   He was suggesting that Aliyah was important, and Aliyah is only to one place.

CD   *The Rebbe spoke to you in Yiddish or English?*

SC   English, even though I do understand Yiddish. But he spoke to me in English, and it was a very unusual meeting in that there was a chemistry that I could feel with the Rebbe. It's as if we knew each other, or had known each other, and we picked up in the middle of a conversation that we left off several years before, even though there hadn't been a conversation several years before. So it was a very interesting experience.

From time to time I would catch a Farbrengen on television, I would listen to him for a while, to see what he would say, and what the message was. So I was aware of what was happening.

My second visit to the Rebbe was after the Crown Heights pogrom. I had not gotten an invitation to come. However, I felt I had to go. I was very upset at what happened, what didn't happen, in the Jewish community. Because nothing happened. And I remember it clearly.

CD   *You're referring to the riots?*

SC   Yes, the riots. It was 2 or 3 days after the riots, and I saw nothing in the Jewish press, and nothing in the general press. I was then the Chairman of the conference of presidents, and we don't get involved in domestic issues, but I couldn't contain myself, and I remember calling up NJCRC, the national Jewish community relations council and saying if you don't come out with a statement, if you don't condemn what just happened, and you don't support our people, I'm going to have to find a vehicle to come out with a statement. I said, this silence is intolerable.

CD   *Was that Malcolm Hoenlein?*

SC   Right, Malcolm and I. But that was my personal feeling, and I would have found a vehicle, if necessary, but at that time I was told that the NY community relations council was working with Lubavitch, with the community, we shouldn't interfere.

CD   *Did you get cooperation from the other Jewish leaders on the Crown Heights issue? I remember that Abe Foxman, as well as others, made statements that were supportive. But at the beginning there was almost nothing. In a sense, were they blaming Lubavitch for causing the riots?*

SC   I don't know. At first I thought there was maybe a fear of reprisal from the black community and then, I thought no, because they're far away from that community and they wouldn't really be affected. If It is fear, it is real for them. To come out and support a really conspicuous Jewish organization that stands out, that was fearful.

You have to be willing to stand up and say, "That's right, I agree with them, or support them in a visible way." But I must confess that I find that is a problem we are facing in general. People are not willing to be in the front and take the heat.

CD   *In the Jewish community?*

SC   Not only in the Jewish community. They'd rather have somebody else do that. The term leadership is used very loosely nowadays. Leaders are supposed to move up front. I believe in "Acharai". I will go and you come with me. People don't have that today. Leaders are afraid. There's a fear that pervades people, except those who are passionate, and some of those are the wrong people, from taking a stance, being firm, and saying this is what I believe. You may not agree with me, but you have to understand what I believe. I think there are leaders who were are either afraid of the political ramifications in New York or of what others will say. [With regard to this issue], I think some of them heard what I hear, which is, it's been taken care of. Lubavitch is going to take care of it themselves.

By the way, that was the second phone call to the New York community relations board. The response to my first phone call was, "It's been taken care of in New York." When I called a second time they said, "Lubavitch is going to take care of it themselves, and we are not going to intercede until they ask us." My answer was, I'm not asking you to take care of the problem for them. I'm asking you to make a statement of support. That's different.

They didn't make a statement even later. It was all very wishy-washy, under the table.

CD   *What exactly did you want to happen?*

SC   I wanted a condemnation by the Jewish community of the type of behavior that took place, and the fact that there should have been a response from the community, of support of those who were offended and assaulted, and, a call from the municipality to understand what really took place there, because the stories were bizarre and distorted, and I just felt we had a role to play. We couldn't leave it just to the community in Crown Heights, it wasn't fair to them. We had to support them. If a Jew is in trouble in Moscow, we're there immediately within 10 minutes, or if there's a problem in Argentina. Why not in Crown Heights? Why not in our own community?

I was assured something was being done. The following Sunday I happened to be in New York. I said to Malcolm, we really should go and offer support, and we went, Abe Foxman, Malcolm Hoenlein and myself. Without asking anyone whether we should or we shouldn't because that was not important. I wanted to see the Rebbe, and I wanted him to understand that we care. That we have a relationship and we care. We may disagree on many things, but at the core, we are Jews, we are part of the Jewish people. We needed to make that statement. He was surprised to see me.

We had called that we were coming, but it was not set up in advance. He thanked me for coming, and then he said something very interesting . He said "you think your work is done?". Now remember, this was after the peak of Soviet immigration , of the Aliyah, because the big numbers came out in 90 an 91. He said, "You haven't finished. You have even more work ahead of you." I ask what he means, "You have even more work ahead of you"? He said "You will see — You will have greater challenges that will come up for you, so you must remain in the positions you're in, and keep working. It's very important. Don't think that you can sit back and rest. You are not at all finished," which was again, a very interesting comment. This was at "dollars" (the Rebbe would distribute dollars for tzedaka every Sunday). Even though it's usually 20 seconds or so he stopped and he took time and spoke to me. He was very encouraging.

CD   *Did he acknowledge or discuss the Crown Heights incident?*

SC   No; however he appreciated my being there. I think he knew immediately why I was there. I told him I came to offer support. One did not have to describe the details to the Rebbe. He knew what people were saying, even if we said it in just a few words. He was unusual, I mean he was discerning in a way that's unusual, very unusual.

CD   *So he keyed in, right away, on the real reason why you came to see him. It was to encourage you to continue helping Russian Jews.*

SC   Yes. He was alluding to the fact that we had gotten out about 350,000 Jews. However there was a far greater number still in Russia and that there was much work to do in bringing those who came, back to Judaism. Because we were then beginning to do work within the former Soviet Union to help those who did identify, or could identify as Jewish, which, by the way, was not supported by a number of people, at that time. There was discussion in the community as to whether we should help develop schools, help develop Yeshivot, or Batei Knesset in a community when we wanted the Aliyah. The position I had taken and the organization had taken, was that we had to do both. Not everyone is going to leave right away, for those who don't leave, let's help them come back to the Jewish people. I think that his sense was, both had to be done, and I had met with the Rabbi in Moscow, at Mirina Rosha Synagogue.

CD   *You mean Rabbi Lazar?*

SC   Yes, Lazar. And he felt that what he was doing was very important, even though at that time there was still some anti-Semitic behavior toward the Jews who were using this building as the shul. I saw the building next door, which was vacant, that they wanted, which is a very good building, as opposed to the building they were in, which was decrepit. We tried to help with the municipality, to get that building for them, but we were not that successful.

CD   *You know that that the Shul you were in was burnt down?*

SC   Yes, I know. It was burnt down later. We called to offer what assistance we could, because we had helped in sending over food, Kosher food, we helped in sending over Matza, we helped in a number of ways, and he would call the national conference, with no difficulty.

There was a working relationship and an understanding. We were supportive. Which by the way people don't understand, how one who is not a follower of Lubavitch can be supportive.

CD   *That was the second meeting with the Rebbe. Did you have a third one?*

SC   Yes there was. The third one was very brief. The conversations, again were not conversations in the normal sense. At each meeting I had the feeling that I was being encouraged, by one who had powers beyond mine to understand what was happening and what was going to happen, encouraged to continue what I was doing. At no point did he say, "Don't do what you're doing, it's not helpful." Each time it was "You have to do more, you have to continue — Don't think that you've completed, or don't think that the challenge is over. " That was the message. The context in each conversation, he made some comment that referred to the political climate at the time, so that I knew he was tuned in to what was happening. That was part of his message to me, to let me know that he understood what was happening, and therefore could suggest to me to continue doing what I was doing, or to focus on what I was doing, which was also very, very interesting, because there are thousands of issues in the world, and hundreds of thousands of people. I was very impressed by that.

CD   *So the third time you met him, was it on any particular issue?*

SC   No, it was still Soviet Jewry. At that time, '92, he encouraged me to overcome the problems. I began to understand that the problems are going to be with those who were coming out who were not knowledgeable of Judaism and did not or would not fit in, and the Rebbe was concerned about what society in Israel would be like.

CD   *Now, a year later, what has happened as far as that?*

SC   It's a difficult issue. I think were looking at a society, and not just Soviet Society, where some, according to Halacha, are not qualified to marry others, and it's going to be very difficult to manage. I think that's one of the difficulties that has been ignored because of the peace process, but if the peace process comes to a positive conclusion in the near term, I mean a year or so, it's going to be a serious issue in Israel, who will be allowed to marry whom, and how they will be declared tref, not acceptable, and what happens to someone when that does happen. How do they feel about the country they chose to come to, or that invited them to come, because in many cases, as you know, we made it attractive for Soviet Jews to come because we needed them. Population is very important. The movement, in addition to the movement of bringing people back to Am Yisroel, was important demographically to Israel. I really believe, and in a sense I think this is what the Rebbe was saying to me in the last visit, that the numbers helped bring about the peace process. The idea of half a million more Jews, together with the possibility of another half a million coming, helped the Arabs understand that Israel still has the upper hand demographically for a while.

CD   *You mentioned the Peace Process. Do you see this now as a positive step, a negative step, or both?*

SC   We had a major conference call because of Arafat's recent statements in which he praises the terrorists and calls for Jihad.

How do you trust someone who calls for Jihad at the same time he says "I want to make peace"?

I remember asking that question of Prime Minister Peres. He said, "Trust is not the issue. Of course we can't trust in the sense of really trusting, because he's said different things at different times. We look at the actions. We measure him by his actions." The actions, or enough of the actions, are moving in the direction that the Peres government believes is a positive way toward a partial peace. I really don't think there's going to be peace in my lifetime. I think there may be a cessation of war, a reduction in serious hostilities, I think in time there will be some modus vivendi but peace the way we define it — I don't think so, not for a long time.

CD   *I have two questions. One is, you mentioned your background is traditional. In what sense?*

SC   I was raised in a traditional setting. The Yomim Tovim, Shabbos.

CD   *My second question is, since you understand very well the traditional side, how is it that you feel the change in the law wasn't worth it for the commotion it was causing? It seems to contradict traditional standards.*

SC   The terminology I used was "disenfranchising hundreds of thousands of Jews."

CD   *What about the hundreds of thousands of traditional Jews, isn't it disenfranchising for them?*

SC   How? They can look at their children and grandchildren and say, my children are Jewish, my grandchildren are Jewish, my family is Jewish, nothing would have changed for traditional Jews, but [what about] the impact that it had on a Jewish leader, Morris Abram, with children that would be considered non-Jewish, because his wife is not Jewish. Others who had intermarriage, not connected with conversion according to halacha, would be looking

47

at a family where the members would be stereotyped or characterized as not Jewish, when in fact they were, and behaved in a Jewish fashion, and belonged to a Jewish religious institution, whichever it was, sent their children through the rituals. These people would be, in a sense, written out of Am Yisroel.

CD   *Did you ever deal with the issue that the non-observant Rabbinate itself does not expose to the potential converts the various options, and the consequences of each of them? The fact that Orthodox conversion is accepted by everyone else, but not vice versa?*

SC   You're absolutely right. The leadership should at least have the menschlichkeit to tell the potential convert, these are the ramifications. I do think that when there is a conversion, or someone who is thinking of conversion, all the options should be made available and the person should know that there will be limitations or restrictions, and in certain areas he or she will not be considered as a Jew, and they should consider.

CD   *You are involved in both sides of the Jewish community — on the one hand with the Lubavitcher Rebbe, and on the other hand with the Reform and Conservative establishment. How do you do it?*

SC   How have I juggled it? I believe one of the strengths of Judaism, in the twentieth century, is that it offers access in various ways. We never had a monolithic approach to Judaism, at least from my understanding of Torah and our history. There were always differences of opinion, which people tried to work out amicably, in some cases did and in others did not, and there were different approaches to what was G-d's law. In the 20th century we have several approaches, and it is not my role to suggest that one is preferred over others. If there are people who wish to affiliate and adhere to Chabad, that's fine, I think it's wonderful.

I want people to be Jewish, and if that is what attracts them that's fine. If it's Conservative, fine. I don't want to close doors to

Jews, I want to open doors. I accept the fact that there have to be parameters. I am hoping that we can work out parameters that would not ostracize or negate part of the population. It is not at all difficult for me to assist Lubavitch in what they want to do, to assist Orthodox or Conservative Reform to do what they want to do, if they're doing it in what I consider a helpful manner to the Jewish people. If their interest is in humanity, in Tikkun Olam, and in education, I help.

I want educated Jews. How they carry out their lives is not my responsibility. If they're educated, so they know the decisions they're making, they know why they're taking the actions, that's critical. The different forms of education should be there. I don't want to lose people because one form does not suit them. And today we're in a society where people choose. There's a tremendous openness here.

CD *Have you succeeded in influencing your colleagues, over the years, in understanding the attitude of the Rebbe? Was it at all a part of the discussions you had with them?*

SC It was not a major part. There is a lack of understanding of Lubavitch as a movement, and a lack of appreciation of the many phenomenal achievements, the dedication and devotion of the Shluchim. I've met them in all parts of the world, and I am fascinated, and very appreciative of what they're doing. Frequently I find that there are offshoots. If they are there, someone can come in and also benefit and assist in reawakening or re-educating Jewishness. I would say that there are not too many who are willing to sit and listen to my explanation or to why I feel that way. If anything the question is how you can work for them, or with them, or assist them. I explain that I don't have to be part of them. I know what the purpose is. It's valid and beautiful and in keeping with my belief in Jewish life.

CD *If you look around the country, how many warm, open, receptive people like yourself are there?*

SC   I'll tell you a very painful story . My eldest son's friend went to a Los Angeles college. He came from a very professional, fine Reform household and fell in, as his mother put it, with Lubavitch. Caught by the cult. That is exactly what she said. She called me up, very upset. Why me? It's true I had known her son, but my role in the community was seen as one that's balanced and serves as a bridge between various groups.

She says her house isn't kosher, it never was kosher, he can't eat there, he's interested in becoming part of the movement. It's a tragedy. My response was, "It's a tragedy? Your son wants to be more Jewish!"

"It's different from our way of life and now my son won't be part of our family. We don' fit in, now he can't come over and eat."

It ended with my coming over to her house, speaking to her and her husband, and assuring them that it's not a cult, don't worry, and there is an understanding on the part of Lubavitch. First of all, she can kosher the kitchen, that's not a big deal, you can buy kosher food that's also good. Second, begin to understand that what he's doing by changing his name from the English to the Hebrew, is wonderful. But it took time, several years, before they could overcome this fear [coming from] a lack of understanding. Those of us who travel around the world have no fear because we see the positive results of the Lubavitch movement.

They do not recognize that it is not much more restrictive than other ways of life. When they see and recognize what is being done throughout the world — I'm thinking of Marty Stein — he and I see and meet throughout the world with wonderful Shluchim. We see the sacrifices and know why they're being made.

I can't tell you how I made it. One of the compliments to my leadership was when I was invited to the Ner Israel banquet. I accepted the invitation knowing I wasn't going to sit at the head table, but then, I know the system. I'm friendly with Rabbi Newberger. I work with him. We have discussions, sometimes debates on issues. When I was invited to address them, as a member of the Federation, that was an achievement, a recognition that we do have a working relationship. Okay, I can't sit at the table, so

I'll sit at the next table. I had a message to bring, of cooperation and togetherness. They invited me and I gave the message. I am not uncomfortable. The OU had a meeting, four, maybe five years ago in New York and invited me to speak. It's because I don't set up barriers. I guess my reputation is OK. I can be invited to the Arbeiter Ring circle or to the Orthodox community.

CD   *What did you see in the Rebbe that is different from other religious leaders? What is his uniqueness?*

SC   His perception. He was able to convey, in practically no words, his knowledge of what I was doing, the responsibility that I had, and where that was going to take us as a people. The other leaders have been focused on their [own] responsibility. The Rebbe was not. He was focused on Jewish community. He brought the larger picture with him always. I had the sense that he was a mystery, he was a vessel . He was doing what had to be done because he felt that this was the critical thing. He did not focus on himself at all. He understood. There's a chemistry when people meet. In my case the chemistry was immediate, I don't know about others. It was as if we knew each other, and we knew what each other were thinking at the time, he far more than I, but I knew what he was thinking also, which is a very interesting sensation, very difficult to describe, but I knew what he was saying. He was speaking in code but I knew exactly what the code was.

I was impressed, also, by the fact that he focused on each individual. He took the trouble and the time to know two people were speaking. Most leaders don't bother to do that. They deal with the issue, but not with the person. It was remarkable. There was a sense, sensory, that he was focusing on the total individual as well as the issue.

The Rebbe was a very unusual person. His serenity, which I have not met in anyone else. His blue eyes, everyone knows, remarkably blue, very clear, and his ability to respond very quickly. I had a feeling that he was 6 or 7 sentences ahead of where I was. But there was a serenity about him which I found very unusual, and I did not attribute it to the fact that he was older, but that this was the Rebbe, And that, in my case, applied to me. I was very comfortable and very relaxed, even though I was in the presence of a very great man, and with other people I would be a little apprehensive. In this case there was this serenity that surrounded him which he was able to transmit or to convey to those who were willing to receive it. I don't know that everyone is going to receive it, but in my case it was very comfortable. I had the feeling that I was in the presence of someone who had a sense of the world more than most people I have met. He was aware of what was happening in many parts of the world, not just because he had communication.

By the way, the Chabad communication system has far surpassed any other facet of American Jewry. I am astounded and also appalled that we have not caught up with Lubavitch.

Seriously, using television and international lines and satellite I think is phenomenal. I was the president when Conference Jewish Federation initiated its satellite capability, which is used very seldom from my perspective. I would like to see Jewish television as an educational tool, if nothing else.

This was an individual who because he didn't focus on himself, was able to focus outward on so many, and to understand that people were looking for ways to be engaged in a more meaningful life. He was able to touch that. Very, very unusual. A unique individual. Even for one who was not a follower, but with tremendous respect for what he did, what he understood, and his ability to recognize the challenges and to work at resolving them.

It's clear that his work continues. I had no doubt about that. There were some who said, "It's going to fall apart," but they did not know the Shluchim, because there is a piece of the Rebbe in each of them and they have the same holy responsibility, so I never doubted that. I don't know how one could be engaged as all of you are engaged, based on one individual's, as great as he was, word. I mean, you yourselves have inculcated that in yourselves. That's not going to change.

4

Professor Zalman Dimetrofsky

Translator Works of Rashba, Former Talmud
Professor (Jewish Theological Seminary)

TALMUDIC SCHOLAR

CD   *Professor Dimetrofsky, I understand you were a professor of Talmud at Jewish Theological Seminary and you worked on the translation of different manuscripts. Can you begin with a brief background of yourself?*

PD   I was born in Israel to a Rabbinic family that goes back to the Vilna Gaon. A great-great grandfather of mine was a very close associate of the Vilna Gaon. The tradition of the Lithuanian Rabbinic study prevailed in the family until today. My father was a Rabbi who came here very young. He married the granddaughter of the Rosh Bais Din of Yerushalayim. He served in the Rabbinate for 60-70 years. He came here around 1910 as a young man, about 18, and he never left Israel until his death, about 27 years ago.

His name was Reb Yaakov Yosef Dzimitrovski. I shortened the name when I came to America and called it Dimetrofsky. Until the age of about 18 I studied in Etz Chaim and then in Mercaz HaRav. Then I decided to get also an academic education, and I went to the Hebrew University. I graduated in 1951. My major was Talmudic studies. I knew him slightly before, but in 1951 Professor Lieberman, the great Talmudic scholar, came for a visit to Israel. He asked me if I would agree to come to teach at the Jewish Theological Seminary, of which he was the director.

I agreed to come, maybe gladly, because I admired him

53

very much. I had not known him personally before, and I was very glad to be in his presence. It turned out to be a very, very happy moment when I met him. We were much, much more than associated, until the day he died. I learned a great deal from him.

This was how I first came to the Rebbe. When Professor Lieberman asked me if I wanted to come to the Seminary, I really didn't know what it was. I imagined it was something like a university where people study and do research. When I came to New York I saw it was not just a scholarly institution, although I was overjoyed with the beautiful library, which is unique in the world. I saw that the institution is involved in many other things, theological things, religious things.   I had some hesitation if I should stay because the Seminary was Conservative and I am Orthodox.

A student of mine was very close to Lubavitch and to the Rebbe, Rabbi Zlotnick. He teaches now at the Seminary. About 1952 or the beginning of 1953 there was a Farbrengen and he came over to me and said, "look, I'm going down to the Rebbe, would you like to come?" I have to say that I was very far from all this. I said, "I'll come down with you." The moment I came in, I thought, "Oh, it's from heaven. I'll ask the Rebbe whether to stay in the Seminary or to go back."

It came out very late, after midnight, after the Farbrengen. The secretary said, "I'll arrange for you to go in." When I entered the Rebbe's room I realized what I was confronting. We spoke in Yiddish. He asked me about myself, and I told him.

Then I asked him the question. I told him I just came a short time ago to the Seminary. His answer was, "As long as Professor Lieberman is in the Seminary, you can stay there. If you resign it won't make a good impression. If he decides to leave, then you leave as well." This was the answer, and I continued to teach there until '78, when I came to the Hebrew University.

This was my first meeting with the Rebbe.

CD   *When the Rebbe said, "As long as he's there" — Is there some history behind that?*

PD   Professor Lieberman never met the Rebbe, but he respected

54

the Rebbe very much. There was a period starting in the late '60s that Lieberman went every summer to Israel. He asked me to take care of his business at that time. I knew there was correspondence between him and those who were close to the Rebbe.

He used to make considerable yearly contributions to all kinds of Chinuch. I know also that in his will, he died 11-12 years ago, he left a considerable amount of money for the various charitable funds of the Lubavitch movement.

The second encounter with the Rebbe was also with this student a few years later. This was Erev Rosh Hashanah. He once again asked me to accompany him. I said I would gladly go. When we came in it was close to one in the morning. There was a big crowd outside. There were so many people ahead of us that I told my student maybe we should go home. One of the secretaries, I think Rabbi Klein, whom I was close to in the later years, told me not to go, he would arrange things. He gave me a hint, I went in. All I had in mind was to get a Brocho and leave.

The Rebbe said "Zitz", sit down. He started to talk about a number of things. The main issue was Korbonos, what the meaning of Korbonos is, what is accomplished by the sacrifice of an animal? He explained that matter can be elevated, what a Korban can do to raise physical matter. He gave a long explanation according to Chasidus. After half an hour I said, "Maybe I should leave", and he replied "Zitz."

He asked me, "How many students do you have?" I figured, since I had two or three classes, I said about 70-80. He said, "If I give each student a minute I still owe you about 40 minutes. I'm not talking to you, I'm talking to the students." I got the message. What he wanted is that I should try to deliver to the students what he was giving me.

At the time of this second yechidus there was much discussion in the seminary about the Korbonos remaining in the siddur. There were those at the seminary who wanted to obliterate it. They felt it was outdated. I believe this is why the Rebbe spent so much time explaining to me the spiritual meaning of korbonos, demonstrating their relevance. This he felt I should communicate to my students as a counter response to those elements who felt korbonos were primitive.

Two or three years later we went down for a Farbrengen. I didn't have in mind to go for Yechidus, I just wanted to be at the Farbrengen. This was on 14 Kislev. It was in the new shul, and the minute I walked in the door, he called me by name and asked me to come up to the platform and say l'Chaim. Immediately there was a "splitting of the sea." I walked up.

Several years later there was something with the family where I needed advice. I had a question at a certain point about staying in American or going back to Israel. I had been at the Hebrew University for a year, on Sabbatical. They were offering me the moon to stay. A very attractive contract. If I may say so, I could write my own.

The difficult point was a commitment I had made to a close relative of my wife. His son had been staying with us in America, a brilliant young man. At that time he was 14 years old, and he had already graduated high school. The best Universities in America wanted him.

His father had asked us to keep an eye on him. He wanted me to steer him in the direction of Jewish learning, Talmud. This had been in the family for generations. Rabbonim, Roshei Yeshivos. While we were in Yerushalayim we enrolled him at yeshivas Kerem BeYavneh. He did not do well at the yeshiva. It was a very frustrating year for all of us, a great disappointment

When my wife and myself, returned to America I had the opportunity to meet with the Rebbe. I poured my heart out about the difficult choice facing me. I had promised this boy's father to help in his development, but he did not seem to be following the family tradition.

The Rebbe suggested that I stay in America, bring him back from Israel and keep an eye on him there, encourage him in learning.

I did not listen. I spent most of my time in Israel, and there was no change in this young man's attitude. He is very successful today, but not in what I would consider a Torah existence. I still feel that I have neglected the trust put in me by not whole-heatedly taking the Rebbe's advice.

Then, whenever we came to America, which was for a long period almost every year, I went down, and each time he gave me a lot of Chizuk. He always remembered the last time. The last time I saw him was two or three months before his stroke. When I told him things, he would answer, "Bekorov Mamash," very soon.

Last year we were in America. I was at the funeral, later I went to his Ohel.

CD   *For a great deal of your life you have kept up a connection with the Rebbe.*

PD   I used to send him all of my books.

CD   *How many books have you published?*

PD   I can show you. You know Mosad HaRav Kook is publishing the "Chidushei HaRashba." This volume is on Tractate Rosh Hashana and Megilah.

CD   *You collect manuscripts, or you explain and add your own insights?*

PD   I explain everything! I printed it from manuscript. The old edition was abridged, and this one is much fuller.

I am now preparing a new edition of the Rashba's Responsa, based on manuscripts. Two volumes have come out already.

Some of his Responsa are answers to difficulties in the Gemora. Not Halachic questions. For instance, this quote: (Professor Dimetrofsky points to a section in the commentaries on the Talmud which doesn't correspond with the Halacha! He explains that this response was probably from the Meiri, and that the Meiri didn't have the original manuscript of the Rashba, therefore he quotes him incorrectly. However in the new edition of the responsa of the Rashba it quotes the same thing; however, now it does correspond to the halacha.)

The Rashba's Responsa came out in such a corrupted state

because the printers did not know the Spanish handwriting. They were not Talmidei Chachomim. They did not know what they were setting.

We had about 4000 Responsa. From what he mentions, he probably wrote twice as much. Let me show you. This is a two-page responsum. In the printed edition all of the reasoning is left out and just the conclusions are printed. That's all they were interested in. The truth is that it is so complicated that the Pri Chodosh, who was a Gaon, writes, "this needs further study".

Everyone, the Bais Shmuel, Rabbi Akiva Eiger, they write on this paragraph in the Shulchan Aruch based on this Rashba, but none of them go back to the source. Boruch Hashem I found the source, that it is Rava who made that statement.

This bothered me so much that I couldn't sleep. One time in Shul I prayed that Hashem should enlighten my eyes, and Boruch Hashem he did, and I found the source of the halacha.

CD   *Do you mean to say that things which are in the standard commentaries are confused and corrupted?*

PD   Not corrupted. They took out the Halachic decision, but the original is a completely different world. They did not have the reasoning of the Rashba himself. I have to give credit to Finkelstein of the Seminary. He helped me do it.

Boruch Hashem I also discovered the "Sridei Bavli."

CD   *What is this?*

PD   Here you have a printing of the Bavli with Rashi. A few pages were known, but nobody knew what it was [(the provenance)]. Boruch Hashem I collected over 500 folios from different libraries all over the world, once I identified what this edition is, I was able to put it together in this book called "Sridei Bavli", which means the remnants of the Babylonian Talmud. In other words, many sections of the Talmud Bavli that are missing, are collected in this sefer. It was detective work. I could only have done it in the Seminary.

The old prints always had a watermark, from the factory where the paper was made. These pages all had watermarks. There was a bibliographer who wrote a book, in which he collected about 30,000 watermarks. It is very important in identifying books. These pages have either of two watermarks. One is a hand, and the other has a combination of a crown and a diamond. These two were not in this man's collection, but they were the key to the whole thing.

The Seminary has a big collection of incunabula, and I was determined to find these marks. There was a Jewish printer Judah Lafara, he had a big establishment for making Hebrew books. The first or second book he printed was the commentary of Radak on the prophets.

I went page by page and found these two watermarks. There was no doubt that this was a Shas printed in 1484 in Spain. This is very important, because Rishonim like the Raavad, Baal HaMaor and the Ramban quote "readings which are found in [printed] books", and this is one of the sources they are referring to.

I sent the Rebbe a copy.

CD   *You are familiar with Manfred Lehman?*

PD   Yes, he collects, but I doubt he has this. It is so rare, that when it became known I was working on it, people started offering a thousand dollars a page.

CD   *You say that the Rebbe told you to stay at the Seminary as long as Professor Lieberman was there. Why did you take his advice?*

PD   I'll tell you why. As much as I could judge, there is such a thing as prejudice. If you went to an Orthodox Rabbi in Brooklyn, the first thing you'd hear would be, "Seminary, oy! Tref! Escape immediately." Here I knew I would get a judgment that you could not attribute to prejudice, a judgment that would be based on what is best for the cause. For example, I could have gone to Reb Moshe Feinstein. Aside from his tremendous learning, he was a very considerate person, and he would not say something without thinking. But still, I knew he was not familiar with the activities of the Seminary, nor with what is going on there. He would be making a judgment between me and the Seminary. However I knew that the Rebbe's judgment would be more comprehensive, litovas hainyan, for the cause. You could see what he had in mind, when he said, "I am not talking to you, I am talking to your students. He wanted that I should become a conduit to transmit the message.

By the way, I left out one detail. At that Yechidus I poured out my heart. I made an indirect remark to the argument between the Baal HaTanya and the Gaon. I said, "Nu, a descendant of the Gaon came now to Lubavitch."

He said "No, he didn't come to me, we are going together, as partners, hand-in-hand."

CD   *He used the words "hand in hand"?*

PD   Yes. This is already years after. He meant, "You are not one of the conservatives, but you represent something else, namely Orthodoxy."

CD   *At the second Yechidus he spoke to you about Korbonos. Did you make a memorandum of what the Rebbe said?*

PD   No.

CD   *There was no correspondence?*

PD   No. I will tell you something else. I sent him every Sefer, and this Sridei Bavli was selling for $400. It is interesting that I did not receive any formal letter acknowledging the receipt of the seforim.

I think the reason for this is that sometimes there's a "hiding of the face" and sometimes there is a "revelation of the face". I had been thanked by him vis-a-vis the "hiding of the face". I knew, for example, a colleague of mine who was, at most, "traditional", an admirer of Rabbi Yehuda Halevi. I don't think he ever studied the Rambam's Yad, but he may have studied The Guide for the Perplexed. I saw correspondence he had with the Rebbe. At first I was puzzled, and then I was very proud.

I explained it like this — this person needs strengthening, and the Rebbe thinks I do not need strengthening. It's enough that I come once a year or so.

Then, my daughter married a Russian who came here. A totally miraculous story. He is a real Yiras Shomayim. His brother-in-law was very active in Russia and here. A year before my daughter got married, his sister and brother-in-law went to Crown Heights. The Rebbe gave them a Brocho, including a Brocho for the brother to get married. The Brocho was fulfilled with in a year.

We sent a fax and an invitation to the Rebbe when they were about to get married. The couple themselves got a very nice letter.

CD   *Now, in your thought process, how do you see the Rebbe?*

PD   I would say that the most striking thing is the width of his knowledge. There is no area where he doesn't have it all in his hand, whether it's Kabbalah, Midrash, Agada, Gemorah, Poskim. Take for example the Rogatchover. He also had this kind of knowledge in Bavli, Yerushalmi, and Rambam, but he did not display it in the other areas, Kabbalah, Midrash. It's all in halacha, and all his knowledge of Agada is only that which is contained in Bavli and Yerushalmi. The Rebbe has no area which is not under his control, "packed in a box".

The second thing is his great ability to throw light from one area to another. To take a halachic concept which looks to be purely logical/analytic, and to apply it immediately to Agadah, and on the other hand, to take an Agadah which seems non-logical, and apply it to explaining a Halachic concept.

It looks like he never had to prepare, or think about it. It just flowed.

CD   *I am sure he spent hours learning it.*

61

PD   Learning it, yes. Nobody can prepare by heart a lecture of five, six hours. You have to create it while you are presenting it. You can have a general line of what you want to stay, but step after step after step you cannot memorize.

I knew people with tremendous memories. My father knew Krisos, Meilah and Erechin like a cheder boy knows "Yeush shelo midaas" [part of tractate Bava Metziah, studied by boys as they begin learning talmud]. When he spoke, he would speak for an hour, but these were things that he had spoken about before, in Yeshiva.

Here you have many topics that were never discussed by anyone, never talked about ever, and it's all set into a chain of reference, of flowing creativity, of new areas of investigation. That's something I have never seen.

Lieberman also had tremendous breadth of knowledge, but I knew that he had to prepare. I can say for sure that no one can talk for an hour and say exactly what he prepared in advance, unless of course he reads it from a page. This is something I have no ability to explain.

CD   *Did he give you any specific advice for the Seminary?*

PD   No. I really thought this was one of his greatness'. He told you what is good, but he never told you what to do. He never said, "Do this" or "Teach this".

CD   *You, and Professor Lieberman, and all the others who were observant of Torah and mitzvos, did you have a strong influence on the Conservatives?*

PD   I don't think we had much influence on the Conservative movement, but we did influence many students. Many students came out frum. For example, I have more than twenty students who made Aliyah and are real Shomrei Torah and Mitzvos. They put on Tefillin. They keep Kashrus very strictly. They educate they children very well.

CD   *And they were not doing these things when they were in the Seminary?*

PD   No. They all came from conservative backgrounds, from outlying places, not from New York. A lot of then were from the Midwest.

CD   *Is there an institute which is supporting your work on Rashba?*

PD   I am alone. Mosad HaRav Kook publishes it. They help me with the footnotes, they look at the galleys, but everything else is mine.

CD   *I wish you success in your work.*

5

Mr. Malcolm Hoenlein

Executive Vice-Chairman, Conference of Presidents of Major Jewish
Organizations

GLOBAL JEWISH AFFAIRS

CD   *Please tell me a little about yourself.*

MH   I am a native of Philadelphia, I grew up there and went to
Yeshiva there . I did my doctoral work in college there. As an
undergrad, I arranged for Avreml Shemtov to come and give a shiur
in Temple University daily, in Gemorah. We had grown up in the
same area.

Even before his arrival, Rabbi Popack arranged for me go
come as a very young child, before Bar Mitzvah, to Crown Heights
for Simchas Torah This was the first time I saw the Rebbe. I was
there when he gave out honey cake, erev Yom Kippur. This is one
of the few things I can honestly say I remember from those years.
His eyes were so piercing. He stopped the line to talk to me and ask
me questions about myself and my family.

I am from a Yekkische background. Seeing Rebbes was not
the most natural thing, but I have a predilection towards it, especially to Chabad. I spent Simchas Torah there for many years.

That year the Rebbe gave me four pieces of lekach to take
home to my parents and my brother. I put it in my pocket. When I
got home they were very impressed by it. What was more impressive was that six or seven years later, when I saw the Rebbe in the
context of some work I was doing, he remembered our earlier meetings.

CD   *What kind of work were you doing?*

MH   Soviet Jewry.

I left Philadelphia in 1971, to be the director of the Conference on Soviet Jewry in New York. After that, from 1976 to 1986 I was director of Jewish Community Relations Council of NY. I worked very closely with Crown Heights on many issues that deeply affected Lubavitch. I was very involved in bringing Professor Branover out of Russia. I arranged to pay for his exit tax. I still maintain a close relationship with Professor Branover.

I maintain a very close relationship with the council and many of the issues we were involved with in those days — police issues, neighborhood issues, security. In 1986 I became director of the Conference of Presidents of Major American Jewish Organizations.

The most remarkable experience I ever had with the Rebbe was in 1991, in the summer. My father was very sick and my son was getting married. I had taken my children to the Rebbe in the years before to get a brochoh. My son's fiance was here that Sunday, and we decided to go. If the line for dollars wasn't too long we would go in. Nobody knew I was coming. I was walking down Eastern Parkway. Someone saw us and told us to come up the front steps. I went up to the front door and opened it. There was the Rebbe.

Rabbi Groner saw me. He went over to the Rebbe and said, "This is Malcolm Hoenlein."

The Rebbe said, I know exactly who it is," and he smiled from ear to ear. His eyes! Rabbi Groner was a little taken aback when the Rebbe said this.

The Rebbe started talking to me about my work. He said, "I follow you very closely. I know what you're doing, you work for Eretz Yisroel, you work for Yidden." I was too stunned to appreciate the significance of it at the moment. This lasted a few minutes. He was very complimentary.

I said to him, "Rebbe, I would like to have a Brocho for my father who is very sick. He said to me, "Your father should continue to have nachas from all the good work you do."

I looked puzzled by his response. He talked to me a little more, and again I asked him for a brocho for my father. He said again, "He should continue to have nachas from all the good work you do."

CD   *What went through your mind when he did not respond directly to your request?*

MH   It was very disturbing that the Rebbe would not give him a Brocho, but more mystifying I could not understand how to read was he was saying. He just patiently responded with some other comment. I had asked for a brocho for my father a few months earlier, but there was no indication that the Rebbe knew how sick he was at that time.

I went to Philadelphia the next morning to visit my father. I was told that he had passed away a short time earlier. My father of blessed memory had an appreciation for the Rebbe, even though he was a real Yekke. He must have had some Chasidische blood.

I have carried the Rebbe's picture with me for many years. I went into Arab countries in the late 60's — I was with the foreign policy research institute, doing many things.

CD   *Any close calls?*

MH   Yes. Once in Russia where I was arrested in 1966. I escaped house arrest in a hotel. The thing I had that was identifiable was a pair of small Tefillin, miniature Tefillin from the Holocaust. Somebody had given them to me to travel with.

CD   *In the 70's you were active with Russian Jewry. Did you correspond with the Rebbe on those issues?*

MH   Not directly. We did have a difference in the total approach to public demonstrations.

CD   *Were you working with Meir Kahane?*

MH   No. I was Director of the Conference on Soviet Jewry. We were the ones who organized the demonstrations on Fifth Avenue with 150,000 people, Solidarity day. We believed in public diplomacy and private diplomacy. As you know, Lubavitch's approach was not to support public demonstrations, but that did not inhibit our ability to communicate with the Rebbe.

We always consulted with Rebbe's and Roshei Yeshiva about different things, and they appreciated and understood why we felt we had to do things the way we did.

There were many other instances. I had been in touch with the Secretariat, Groner, Krinsky, and others, even more so later on.

I consulted on a complex issue that had to do with whether I should take my present position. The Rebbe himself expressed the view that I had a choice of two positions to take. JCRC or the President's conference.

CD   *Did you discuss the differences between the Rebbe and the President's Conference?*

MH   I had the opportunity to go in to the Rebbe about personal things, illness in the family, once about Soviet Jewry. I knew what Lubavitch had done when no one else was there. They were often a source of information about people or things which had to be done to get people out of trouble.

CD   *The library?*

MH   Even early on. The seforim in Moscow.

CD   *Not the ones which were taken and returned in the US?*

MH   No, although when I was at JCRC there were many times where we helped problems with the city and the state.

CD   *In California, for an Orthodox Jew to be in a leadership position is very rare. New York is more traditional, but how is it that you have this position? Does the Reform movement allow you in?*

MH   The fact is that when I came in to this field I made a decision to do this, having been involved in Kiruv and other things.
When I come to NY for the Soviet Jewry conference, one very
impressive person, I think it was Gershon Jacobson, said, "Don't
worry. In six months no one will remember you." The corollary
story with that was that they said, "He's young, the young people
won't work with him, he's frum, the frum people won't work with
him, he's an activist, and the activists won't work with him, he's a
Zionist, and the Zionists aren't going to work with him." Boruch
Hashem we proved them wrong. We had a staff of three. All three
of us had to be frum, because who else would be willing to do this?
It was very important to us as religious Jews. We were willing to
be moser nefesh at a time when it wasn't popular, and we built a
movement from the grass roots up.

Then, when the JCRC was formed, I was the natural candi-
date for it. It started with tremendous pains. People said we needed
it like another PLO, it would bring the Ku Klux Klan in to the
Jewish community. The truth is that there had been a tremendous
division between the Manhattan leadership and the rest of Jewry.
Some of them had never even visited communities like Flatbush
and Borough Park.

I took the whole leadership and brought them around to
visit Rebbe's, the Satmar Rebbe, the Lubavitcher Rebbe, the
Bobover, Rabbi Soloveichik, to the Seminary, to give them an
exposure to the community. I think we were able to put some substance in, to put these leaders in contact with them as real people
with issues from day to day.

That gave substance to the JCRC. Then, when I came up for
the position at the presidents' conference, there were many candidates. It was done in a short period of time because I had to make
a decision between this and another position. Despite some concerns about a guy with a yarmulke in that position, they decided to
hire me.

By the time it came to the Presidents' Conference, people
knew me already. I had been in New York, in responsible positions,

for a long time. The truth is that there was a revolution. When we came in it would have been almost unthinkable for Orthodox Jews to occupy the positions they occupy today.

We had to be as good or better. Prejudices. I spoke for 45 minutes about what it meant to be an Orthodox Jew. I was told, "What about Saturday? It's an important day for meeting with our non-Jewish Colleagues."

I asked him, "Is it not G-d's Sabbath for you and I? What about your self-respect?" and I walked away.

Subsequently they called me and made me an offer.

Things have changed a lot. It has been difficult at times. Divisive times, breaking down according to those ideological lines. There are times when I think it is more difficult. I think that people judge you by what you do, by your menschlichkeit. I would say that I have had an incredibly positive experience.

You can have influence, but you have to do it in the right way. The burden of proof is on you, not on the others. If you demand respect you're not going to get it.

I was spared some of it. At the Presidents' Conference we don't deal with Halachic issues, as it was at the JCRC. But there are many difficult and divisive issues, especially now.

CD   *What is the mission of the Presidents' Conference?*

MH   It is the largest umbrella of the American Jewish Community. It covers fifty national Jewish organizations, from left to right. UJA, Council of Jewish Federations, AIPAC, American Jewish Committee, American Jewish Conference. The OU is a member, Young Israel is a member.

CD   *They look to you for direction?*

MH   We deal only with national and international issues. We do not deal with domestic, local issues. We deal with global things that affect Jewish security directly, from the boycott to legislation in Congress.

CD   *Back to when you were 12 years old, when the Rebbe stopped the line.*

MH   Many people he just would give it to, and they would go. But me he stopped, and started talking. I felt that he was looking right through me. I was pretty mesmerized.

He asked about my family. People started running up to see who he is talking to, a little nothing of a kid. There is an aura about the Lubavitcher Rebbe. I felt it as a child. The Rebbe has a very special quality. His questions were always penetrating. His incredible ability to recall and know somebody from many years before, and to relate in that way. Why would the Rebbe know what I was doing? There's no reason in the world to expect that the Rebbe should be so familiar, able to talk with me about it with such warmth, such clarity, such knowledge and familiarity.

I am thinking about when I came in '91. I had been involved in so many things. This is a very special quality that one doesn't find. When you meet great people, they can be great by virtue of their position and title, the setting in which they find themselves. My parents weren't Misnagdim in the classical sense, in fact we davenned in a shtiebel later on, but we did not grow up with Chasidus. I was very attracted to it. I was attracted to the warmth of Lubavitch, to the Kiruv work, to the outreach, to much of what it stood for and what the Rebbe taught.

It was something very special. That experience as a 12 year-old was incredible. Nobody had a chance to tell him. Nobody knew I was coming. I didn't know I was coming.

6

Rabbi David Hollander

Rabbi Hebrew Alliance of Brighton, Jewish Press Columnist, Former President
Rabbinical Council of America

KEEPER OF TRADITION

CD *Rabbi Hollander, can you give a brief description of how
your relationship with the Lubavitcher Rebbe developed?*

DH First of all, I want to thank you for the opportunity to give
this interview, and hopefully it will be LeShem Shomayim, and it
may help people themselves to be influenced by the teachings of
the Rebbe zt"l.

    I personally came to the Rebbe on the rebound, in 1955. I'll
get to that later, but I must tell you also that I saw the Rebbe, without having any contact with him, on the day of his arrival. I was at
the pier in the New York harbor. They arrived on a ship which was
practically the last to leave Europe.

CD *Was it the Rebbe or the Previous Rebbe you saw?*

DH First came the Previous Rebbe, in 1940, and I was there.
That day was bitterly cold and there were relatively few people
there. Then came the Rebbe, in 1941, I'm quite sure I was there as
well. That was a very critical time. I remember one thing which the
previous Rebbe said on the day after he came. He made the
announcement that "America is not different." That was the slogan
that was followed. I had occasion to repeat this many time around
the world, when I spoke about the phenomenon of Lubavitch. I told
them this because this is the quintessence of the whole idea — if

71

you put your mind and your heart to it, LeShem Shomayim, you can accomplish things. But he said it at a time when his most ardent followers could not believe it.

He had very few followers left here in America, very feeble as an organization. There was a Rabbi Jacobson Zecher LeBrocho and a few others, and they did what they could, but everything was against them in this country.

CD   *How did you know about the Previous Rebbe? Did you have a relationship with any of his Chasidism?*

DH   One of my traits is curiosity. This idea that a Rebbe is coming from Europe, especially at that very critical time! I went out of curiosity, and possibly out of Derech Eretz for a Godol Hador, but not as a Chasid. I was not anywhere near a Chasid. I don't think I was ever a true card-carrying Chasid. You have to have a certain self-nullification to be a Chasid, where you don't have any questions, you don't ask anything.

I had many times Yechidus with the Rebbe, which always lasted more than an hour. On one occasion, after I was already close, he said to me, "I heard you have complaints about me." I said, out of Derech Eretz, "No, no complaints, but I don't understand." So he said, "Let's talk about it." He called me in and we talked about it.

CD   *What was your background?*

DH   I came to America as a child from Hungary, before my Bar Mitzvah. My father Zichrono LeBrocho was a Rov in a town in upstate New York. He came to America before the family, as was customary. He was not a Chasid , but he was not a misnaged. I know he had a great reverence for the Karestirer Rebbe. My father went to him occasionally, and my mother comes from a town which is known for a great Rebbe, the Kalaver Rebbe.

Certainly we were not Chasidism, but we were not Misnagdim in any sense of the word. My early connection was to my teachers in Torah Vodaas and Yitzchok Elchonon, where my

Rebbe was Reb Yoshe Ber Soloveitchik, and his father Reb Moshe. There was a Rav Aranovitch, Zecher Tzaddik LeBrocho, a great Talmid Chacham, who signed on the ordination of those who were ordained there. I had no connection with Chasidic Rebbeim directly. I had heard about the Lubavitcher Rebbe, as many people had.

I did not go to him to seek his guidance and help until a certain spiritual crisis came into my life. I was the president of the Rabbinical Council of America, Histadrus HaRabbonim, in 1954. I was a rebel against the established trend of the organization, which was modern orthodoxy. The issue I raised at that time, which stirred up everyone very strongly, was the issue of associating with Conservative and Reform leaders, in a Rabbinic organization, as distinguished from being with them in a general Jewish organization.

The members of the Rabbinical Council of America belonged to various Boards of Rabbis, which also included various Conservative and Reform Leaders, all of them flaunting their violation of Jewish law and claiming that this was "Twentieth Century Judaism". It was incredible to me that one could belong.

They had figured I would cool off when I was elected president. As soon as I was elected, I asked one of the members what I should do. I wanted to do something. He said, "Do nothing. If you do nothing you'll be a great success." I did not take the advice.

There was a great Godol Hador at that time, best not to mention his name, with whom I was very, very close. I was disillusioned in his inability or unwillingness to take a clear stand publicly one way or the other. To me, this was a very disillusioning thing. I was very close to him and I looked up to him. I was very honest, and told him that I was unable to accept his status.

I was looking for some support. I heard about the Rebbe. I had heard that many people went to him, and I was in need of an anchor.

CD   *So you were disappointed with this Godol's opinion.*

DH   No! With his lack of opinion. Even if he had taken a stand opposite mine, I could have accepted that he is a bigger Lamdan, he knows more than me and that's it. Let me put it this way. Everybody learns a certain sincere approach to Torah in the Cheder. Unfortunately, later it changes. Pragmatism takes the place of idealism . My image of a Talmid Chacham, then and now, is, as the Gemorah says, "His yes is yes, his no is no, and there is no weakness." You can say that's too much to expect. Maybe it's too much to expect from a Talmid Chacham like me, but from a Godol HaDor..?

I used that standard. I didn't act quickly, I weighed it in my mind back and forth until I came to the conclusion that I cannot go along. The Mishne says, "Make yourself a Rav, and get away from doubt." If he can't get you out of doubt, then you don't have a Rav.

I went to the Rebbe. I told him I was coming to him because I had this situation, that I am dealing with a Gaon. He knew who it was without my telling him. He told me then — merely understand at that time the meaning of his brief comment — "In our time, everyone must be a Gaon." It obviously meant that you cannot find people today on whom you can say you are going to rely. It's not that kind of a world.

From that point on I never did anything significant without asking the Rebbe. I became a Ben Bayis there. When I came to see the Rebbe, and Rabbi Groner would push the bell, the Rebbe would say, "Zitz, zitz." An hour or an hour and a half was the usual time of the Yechidus. Not for personal matters, though the Rebbe did ask me how I was, but always community matters, Klal Inyonim. First, this question, which later became a tremendous issue. When I raised it within the Rabbinical Council of America there was a tremendous opposition, indescribable, but nevertheless I forced them to have a session of the Vaad Halachah on that subject. This particular Godol Hador was one of the leaders of this session, he told me he wanted me to do everything I could to succeed, then I saw a certain hesitancy. I'm the kind of Jew who couldn't take that [hesitancy]. Maybe others can, but me not.

CD   *So what was the Rebbe's opinion on this issue?*

DH   The Rebbe always told me, with increasing strength, never to relent on this issue, never to compromise. Inside the organization, as president, I was a nirdof, a hunted man. I was not only criticized, the opposition was very hostile. I was no longer a part of the "complexion" of the Rabbinical Council, and of Yeshiva University, which was my school, where I had received my ordination.

There was another issue inside the RCA at the time, in which I took a very strong stand. This is the very critical question of the mechitzos in the congregations. Back then it had a completely different meaning from now. There was a connotation of going back to the ghetto, old-fashioned, Anti-American, and all that.

I was fighting a battle specifically not to allow the Rabbis of the RCA to take congregations where there were no Mechitzos. This affected people's positions and careers, and there was an idea that one was driving people out of the shul by making such requirements. I was what you would call a black—hat right-winger, who had to be watched carefully, and they watched me very carefully. It was bitter.

There was a time when they even tried to impeach me. One very prominent Rabbi, no longer with us, tried to have me impeached. They didn't have any desire to keep me any longer than they were required by their constitution. According to that, you are elected for one year. Then you are customarily elected for a second year, and then you are finished.

They had trouble with me the first year, and they tried to impeach me. They also tried very hard to prevent my reelection by electioneering and putting up other candidates, but it didn't work because it wasn't pursued relentlessly. They figured that by the second year I would already calm down.

CD   *On the issues of Hishtatfus, (formal affiliation with Reform and Conservative leaders) and Mechitzah, what was the outcome?*

DH   On the Mechitzah, the issue won. There is a book, The Sanctity of the Synagogue, in which I have some articles. At that time, strangely enough, the Rabbinical Council per se and some of its ultramodern left-wing orthodox Rabbis, mamash on the border, joined Boruch Litvin, Zichrono LeBrocho. Zecher letov, he did an incredible job. It was from Heaven that he succeeded.

This issue was won, at least theoretically. Subsequently Rabbis were sent to non-Mechitzah shuls only for Kibush Hakehilos, to conquer the community for Orthodoxy. Theoretically, you could only go to such a congregation with the consent of the Roshei Yeshiva, and you had to leave if you did not show results after a certain time. That was in theory only. After a while, instead of the Rosh Yeshiva sitting down himself and interviewing the guy as to whether he was the person to be trusted, someone else did it.

The other battle, the battle against affiliation, was unrelenting. They fought tooth and nail against it. You have to understand, that you had the greatest people of that time, Reb Moshe zt"l, Reb Aron Kotler, and even people on the staff of YU, like Reb Dovid Lifshitz, Zecher Tzaddik LeBrocho, and the son in law of the Chofetz Chaim, who signed on a halachic judgment that it was completely forbidden to join with these organizations. They were strong and unequivocal. It didn't help.

I tried each and every year at the conventions to bring up this issue again, until they adopted some kind of a regulation that you can't bring it up anymore. I don't want to talk about people who are nebech no longer with us, but without mentioning names, I can tell you a humorous thing that happened.

At the convention, no one believed I could be elected, because my issue was an open book to them. It was a hot fight. At the last minute they didn't believe that there was a chance that this upstart would win. Rationally I should not have won. Rabbi Soloveitchik was 100% in my corner, openly, and they held it against him more or less his whole life. He told me only 7 years before his passing, "Up to now they have not forgiven me!" To them, the biggest sin is to go against the apparatus, the establishment. Never mind the principles, the apparatus becomes, forgive the word, the idol to which you bow down.

I can tell you, I was president of the RCA for two years, that was the maximum, and I have not been on the program of a convention for nearly 40 years.

CD   *Because they didn't ask you?*

DH   Because they didn't ask me! Not even to sweep the floor.

CD   *What was the second issue you took up with the Rebbe?*

DH   This was not an issue, but a great historic experience in which the Rebbe guided me every step of the way. It was my trip to Russia. I took advantage of my presidency, so to speak. I went to Washington late in 1955, when my term was coming to an end, and people would soon be celebrating. Rabbi Soloveitchik begged me to stay for a third term, and told me that the constitution would be amended in my favor. He felt that the Rabbinical Council of America was a better thing, because I was there.

He wanted a price from me, that I should momentarily put this issue on the side, and when my position would be stronger I could put it through. I couldn't accept that. It was Purim time. As Mordechai said to Queen Esther, "Perhaps it was for such a time as this that you attained to royalty," — I was there so I could put an end to this affiliation thing then and there. That I should come back and say, "OK boys, forget about it", would make the wrong impression.

Therefore I went to Washington and I was there, ready to go back to New York, when it just occurred to me that the Jews in Russia could not be contacted. This was the accepted thing. Nobody in the big organizations was doing anything.

I took a taxi to the Russian Embassy. I expected to be thrown out, but on American soil what could they do? In those days, just to get through the door! I came in, and I told one of the flunkies, a nobody, maybe a tenth-in-command. I told him that I wanted to speak to someone about a group of Rabbis visiting the Soviet Union. You have to think how out of the question this sounded in those years.

The guy excused himself, and when he came back he said, "Please sit down." I sat down, and a higher flunky came to see me.

I told him what I had in mind. I was very surprised that he took down the details of who we are, where we are located, where our office is. He said he would get back to us. I didn't expect him to get back to us. At all!

They got back to us. They sent us a letter, which I still have somewhere, inviting us to come to the Soviet Union to visit the Jewish communities. At that time the newspapers wrote about it with greater headlines than they write about anything nowadays. It was a breakthrough! America and Russia were hardly on speaking terms!

After a few months a letter came, and the names of the people I submitted were on the letter. To these people visas would be issued. When that happened, I cannot tell you. The New York Board of Rabbis, I thought they were ready to commit suicide. At that time the Orthodox community was nobody in America. They had no place in public life, they were just "nochshleppers", little people. Now, the Orthodox Union has a representative in Washington, as do Agudas Yisroel and Lubavitch; they all have their own people. Then it was another picture entirely. Orthodox people were considered poor relatives. And then, for orthodox Rabbis to make such a scoop!

It was, mamash, a fire. Even the Rabbinical Council of America itself, which was the beneficiary, was not overly happy. They couldn't say so, just like the Israel government now is against Jerusalem becoming the capital, but it isn't nice to say it.

I came to the Rebbe and I told him what happened.

CD   *You were bothered by the opposition?*

DH   No, not in the least. I was worried whether we might cause some hurt, that maybe our going would have repercussions on people in Russia.

The Rebbe told me in the following words, "If you had come to see me earlier, I am not sure what I would have advised you, but now I am sure you must go. Having made the request, you cannot go back on it." I spoke to other Gedoilim, Reb Aron, Reb Moshe, but the main one for me was the Rebbe. Not because I am a Chasid, but because the Rebbe knew Russia better than anyone else. I also believed the Rebbe to be a great Tzaddik and a great Ish Emes [Man of Truth].

I also had good contact with the Satmar Rebbe zt"l on that basis, not that he knew Russia, but his quality as a person and as a Talmid Chacham. He knew I belonged to Mizrachi, and he never asked me to drop out, but you can rest assured he let me know his opinion. I was very close with him.

I was Rabbi of one of the biggest synagogues in America, Mt. Eden Jewish Center in the Bronx. I had tremendous Zionists in my shul, and they said me, "How is it that you can attend an event given by the Satmar Rebbe?"

I said, "Why do I go to the Satmar Rebbe? Because if a man is willing to close up shop rather than to change his principles, I have to look up to him."

Ben Gurion told me the same thing in a different way. He said to me, "What kind of Landsman are you? [What is your family origin in Europe?]" He spoke Yiddish to me! I told him I was ashamed to tell him. He said, "Why are you ashamed?" I told him, "I am of Hungarian descent." He said, "Why are you ashamed?" I said, "Because the Neturei Karta are Hungarians." He said to me, "I respect the Neturei Karta more than the Mizrachi! I know one thing, whatever the Neturei Karta say today they'll say tomorrow, but the Mizrachi I don't know."

The idea is that people were at different extremes, but they had a respect for truth.

CD   *What was the Lubavitcher Rebbe's role in your trip?*

DH   He told me to go, and then he advised me, point by point. First, since I am on an American passport, I am not taking a chance, but the Jews who may talk to me are. Be careful. He said to me, "If you say a sermon in Shul, you must understand you are going back to America, but those people listening may be held accountable — Why did you let him speak? Why did you associate with him. Just because you are an invited, doesn't mean that everything you say and do will be considered kosher for the people there. Don't think the Russian policy has to be consistent."

I was there eight times after this initial visit in 1956, and the Rebbe would caution me, "Don't [necessarily] say what you want to say! You are the one who is safe." I remembered that.

He told me that Lubavitchers would come over to talk to me. "They will be careful, but you should be careful too. Don't act like you know them well, or you know me." This was only three years after Stalin died. Khrushchev was in power, but a lot of things hadn't changed.

There were five people on our delegation. I was the chairman. By that time the convention had taken place, and I was no longer the president, or rather just a lame duck. The people on my delegation were themselves still against me.

CD   *Then why did you choose those people?*

DH   I am a guy who goes by the book. These were officers of the organization. After the fact it was a good idea. If it had not been for them, the whole delegation would not have left, because people were trying to undo it after we were already invited.

The New York Board of Rabbis suddenly announced they were going to Russia. They were not invited by the government, they went to a travel bureau. Nothing I could do about it. But two members of my delegation, especially one, conspired to give the New York Board of Rabbis an official standing. It did not succeed, but he tried. In fact, I brought him up on charges within the organization when we returned, but he had too many people backing him up. Nothing new to me, I'm accustomed to that.

The New York Board of Rabbis came. It was not organizational opposition that bothered me. The more the merrier! What bothered me is that these people were more interested in the political issues than the spiritual. I felt that the entire purpose of our trip should be to bring more Yiddishkeit to Russian Jews.

CD   *What did he do to conspire? He was on your delegation, he agreed to go with you.*

DH Right! And he delayed his own departure on some excuse, to be there when they arrive, knowing that I would not be too friendly, to put it mildly.

We departed, and on the way we stopped off in Amsterdam, because the Israel government was very interested in our trip. To such an extent, that they sent a special ambassador to meet us in Amsterdam, to tell us what to inquire about. We're not talking about the government they have now, we're talking about the original Zionists, who wanted to get together as many Jews as they could, not to separate from the Jews in the Diaspora. An American newspaper also sent a special correspondent. It was a big thing.

We found that the New York Board of Rabbis was also going to arrive in Holland a few days after we got to Russia. They were going to have a reception, and award a certificate to the local Rabbi and they called themselves in Hebrew, "Chaver HaRabbonim"!

So I told the Rabbi who they were, and when they came they were not received, because I had alerted him that they had nothing to do with Torah Judaism; their primary interest was political, not spiritual. The Chief Rabbi didn't know. These movements had become important in America after Russia was already closed off to the west.

It's a long story, which may never be fully told, but the upshot is that one of the members of our delegation left in a huff, and started courting publicity by giving an ugly report of conditions over there, which violated the trust we had with the Russian government. The whole idea was to do a little something for them, in exchange for our being able to help the Jews. I said, and the American ambassador there agreed with me, that we must say that there are still certain sides of Jewish life in the Soviet Union, it is not all terminated as some people may think, and so on, and not to give the impression that there was nothing, because it wasn't true!

This man gave an opposite report. When we went from Russia to Rumania, the chief Rabbi, Rabbi Rosen met us and said, "How come you said a thing like that." We told him it was not us. He sent a telegram from Bucharest to the United States, saying that we disavowed this statement

As I said, the Rebbe told us to be cautious. When I was there, I met Lubavitcher people. People would come up to me in a shul, as I would march with the Sefer Torah. When they bent over to kiss the Sefer Torah, they whispered, "How is the Rebbe? What will be with us." The Rebbe, the Rebbe!

I was in a town called Sukumi by the Black Sea. The local Sefardic Rabbi made a gathering for us. There was a little more freedom than in the other parts of Russia. I saw a Jew sitting at the table who was white like a sheet. I later found out that he had been released from 20 years of prison. Under the table someone handed me a crumpled piece of paper. I put it in my pocket. It turned out to be a letter to the Rebbe. As a result of this, this man, whom you probably know, came out of Russia at a time when nobody came out.

CD   *Who was that?*

DH   Reb Leizer Nanas. He wrote a couple of seforim. He was the man. How the Rebbe did it? I know only part, maybe you can find out. Somebody attended a wedding in Poland from Russia and was handed a note for Nanas from the Rebbe that said not to give up, to keep asking for a permit again and again.

I was in Riga on a subsequent visit. In Riga was Yisroel Pewsner. I wanted to talk to him. My question was, how am I going to identify him? I don't know him by sight and I can't inquire. During the davenning, you are allowed to davven, someone was walking up and down. He knew I was the visitor, because I looked different, so when he passed me I said "Shma Yisroel". He understood I was hinting at his name. But everyone was watching! The local Jews, emissaries of the government, everyone! They were wearing Taleisim and they were watching!

Friday night after davvening I was going to go back to the hotel, where I had my sardines, wine and challah. Everyone left before me, and I was alone for a few minutes. As I left I looked here and there, and I saw him a block away. He made a sign, and I followed him. When I think of it right now it is scary. I wasn't in NY, I was in the lion's mouth. Eyes all over. He waited, when I came up, he walked another block, and another block. After many blocks he stopped and started to cry, "What does the Rebbe say? What will be with us? What will be with us?!"

What other Jew in the world could they relate to? Only the Rebbe.

He showed me a few houses where the Jews lived, and the curtains were drawn so that no one could see that the lights were lit for Shabbos. He finally came to his house, and knocked on the door according to a code. The Shabbos candles were almost finished, we sat down and ate something in the dark. He couldn't walk with me. He just pointed the direction, and I had to walk on my own.

As I approached the hotel, I saw a lot of Russian bums hanging around, and they began to chase after me. I ran with all my strength and just made it to the door of the hotel.

The main thing is, they wouldn't tell me how to find them, but on a Sunday I found them learning a shiur in Gemorah. They were shocked and upset that I came, but I came. Friedman, Pewsner, Notke and Gordin, people like that were there. I took a picture, I put it in my pocket, and when I came I brought it to the Rebbe as part of my report.

The Rebbe said to me, "Tell me, what did you say in your sermon?" He wanted to know, because he had cautioned me. The parsha at that time had been Chukas-Balak. I told the Rebbe, "And Balaam rose up early in the morning, and Rashi says that he was told, 'You evil person. The wise man [Abraham] has already preceded you, [who got up early in the morning for the binding of Yitzchok, in the merit of which the Jews will not be hurt by you].'" The Rebbe told me, "You smuggled in the real stuff!" I myself had thought it was a rather diplomatic way to tell the Jews to have hope.

On my other trips, afterwards, the Rebbe told me to go to Samarkand. I went everywhere, that's why I had such long Yechidus'n. There was so much to discuss.

CD   *Could you talk a little about what you saw in the Rebbe as a leader of the generation, someone who had an impact on a global level? You've been with the best, and I'd like your impressions.*

DH   There is no doubt that there is no one else, that I know of, who has had such an impact on so many people, Jewish people, as the Rebbe has. I say that because no other Rabbi, Yeshiva organization, even secular organization, had the genius that the Rebbe had.

The Rebbe had, in my mind, two tremendous innovations, or maybe only one, looked at from two sides of the coin, which nobody else has.

The concept of having shluchim in the farthest corners of the world is absolutely original. I know in Israel that there were Yeshivas who asked their students to take a job in a small town, even though they would have preferred to be in Yerushalayim. But the Rebbe has an army. The Rebbe says to Dalfin, "I don't want you in Los Angeles. I want you, in Oshkosh, Wisconsin." Dalfin says, "The Rebbe wants me," and Dalfin's wife says, "All right, nu, I'm going along." How do I know that? When Rabbi Yitzchok Groner had a fine job all set up for him in Brooklyn, and the Rebbe said to him, "Go to Melbourne, Australia," and he went!

Yitzchok Groner and a hundred others, a thousand others, left their preferred place, where they were all set with their families and uncles and aunts, and went "there" to make it a place of Torah.

You have to understand that I was directly and personally instrumental in establishing Lubavitch in Australia. The Lubavitcher chasidism came to Australia right after the war. I came there in the early 1950's. I was not a guest of Lubavitch at that time, for the simple reason that Lubavitch was not in a position to invite anybody. I was a guest of the world-famous school, Mt. Scopus. There the principal was going around without a Yarmulke! Nu. The Rebbe had told me to go there to speak. They had inquired of various people, for someone to come and assist them.

CD   *Right, they probably heard of you because of your involvement with the RCA. Therefore they inquired about you as a speaker.*

DH   The RCA??!!! The Rebbe himself was instrumental in my

going to Australia. They had inquired of him directly.

When I came there I had Boruch Hashem success. A delegation from Sidney asked if I would come and do the same thing six months later, which I did. I came to Sidney. There I met Sir Bessin, very rich, totally divorced from Yiddishkeit. Even the local equivalents of our Federation charities he gave little to. Instead he gave to the Universities. I got a call from one of the Feiglins in Melbourne saying that Mr. Bessin is a wealthy Jew, and in Melbourne they need a place for the Bais Rivkah school to meet. This was $100,000 Australian dollars they needed then, about like a million dollars today.

CD   *They wanted you to ask him for $100,000?*

DH   It sounds ridiculous, but Min Hashomayim everything can be. I made contact. He made an appointment with me for a Friday afternoon. First, he wanted to show me what he is. He picked me up in his Rolls Royce and took me to the University, where the professors were lined up to receive their benefactor. Here it was, three-four hours before Shabbos, and this guy is putting on his whole act. Finally I suggest that it's almost the Sabbath, I have to get to the hotel, there is something I want to discuss with you.

He says, "let's go to my office."

I tell him, "There is a group of Jews who came out of Europe after the war, they suffered, they came to Australia, and they haven't got a place for their children to have a school. The little girls have no place to go to school, and I thought I would ask you for your help. They have to buy a building..." I figured he would say, "Here's a hundred dollars, now let me be," which would be a natural thing to do.

Here's a miracle from heaven. He asks me, "What is the name of the school?" Just these words.

I forgot the name of the school, Bais Rivkah. It wouldn't come in to my head. But I remembered the name of a school in the Bronx, Bais Miriam, so I said "Bais Miriam."

"Miriam! That's my wife's name! How much do they need?"

Just like that. This is how it happened. He rings a bell on his desk, a secretary, not Jewish, walks in, and he asks him, "What do you think of this American Rabbi, who's asking me to give this money to these Polish Jews?"

He says, "Mister Bessin, you couldn't do a better thing in your life."

It is just before Shabbos, and I want to clinch the deal. I call up Mr. Feiglin in Melbourne from the office, Mr. Bessin instructs him to come to him on Sunday morning to pick up the check, and that's it.

Sunday morning 7 am, three hours before the Melbourne people are due to arrive, I get a phone call at my hotel. Mr. Bessin he says, "You know, I have a lot of trouble because of you. Someone told me over the weekend, 'You know, you made your money in Sidney. Why are you spending it in Melbourne?'"

What am I supposed to say to that?! I was silent for a moment.

He says back, "Listen, no one is going to tell me how to spend my money."

They came from Melbourne, he put up the money, and they put up the building, Bais Rivkah. Even though his wife's name was Miriam, the school is called Bais Rivka. After that he gave much more money.

CD   *Do you remember my wife's family, Serebranski?*

DH   He lives there, across the street.

CD   *Do you remember his father, Zalman?*

DH   Certainly!

CD   *Gimel Tammuz [the Yahrtzeit of the Lubavitcher Rebbe] was his Yahrtzeit also.*

DH   A fine man, a shining face.

CD   *I heard once that the Rebbe recommended to Shluchim that they invite you as a guest speaker. Did the Rebbe ever discuss speaking for Lubavitch events?*

DH   Yes, the Rebbe did, and this is for the record. It was many years ago. The Rebbe heard about my talks, and maybe even heard some of them, because when I spoke for Lubavitch in New York they would keep a telephone line open to him.

I have been debating, for years, people belonging to the conservative and reform movements, on the radio. I had cases where the moderator, a non-Jew, was on my side, because he couldn't take the hypocrisy.

CD   *You saw two things in the greatness of the Rebbe. One was his sending out Shluchim. The other?*

DH   The other was that the Rebbe, practically alone, took up controversial issues in public and stuck to them at great cost to himself and his movement.

CD   *Such as?*

DH   The question of Mi Yehudi, Who is a Jew? Beyond all this, and probably the foundation of the whole thing, is the fact that there is an address in Brooklyn, and a telephone number, that a person in great trouble can contact. Maybe there is another such a person, but I have never heard of it. Do you know what it means, when you are in a terrible dither, it could be an operation, a marriage, a family problem, business troubles, political plans, seeking office. Everyone felt that if he wanted to, he could find a place there to inquire.

Where do you find today anything like this? People are busy. They can't even say hello to you. A great Rebbe once said, "There is going to come a time when people won't even have a sigh to spare for the next guy. They'll want everything for themselves." That's the time we're living in now.

I want you to know, when I came out from Lubavitch at two

in the morning last week after they celebrated writing a sefer Torah in honor of the Rebbe, I saw something in the street which I may write about. A big streamer was hanging over Eastern Parkway. It said, "July 29 — Love Yourself Parade." The line underneath said, "Stop the Violence".

"Love Yourself Parade." I had just came out of a place where they had completed writing a Torah, where it says, "Love your fellow man as yourself", and here was the contrast in the same neighborhood. "Love Yourself Parade."

To come back to the subject of the Rebbe's shluchim. The idea that Chasidim who dare to wear long coats could be stationed on the door of a University with a Chabad House, is beyond understanding. Modern orthodox Jews, in sport jackets, no beard, no peyos, people like me, the students could relate to, but chasidim would seem to turn them off. And yet the shluchim inspire them and bring them closer!

The Rebbe was unique.

"Don't be modest against my account", is what the Rebbe said. "Modesty has nothing to do with teaching the word of the Torah. You should be interviewed by the papers, state your views, make yourself known when you come to a place." This is not the way I was brought up, I never put myself forward, but if the Rebbe said it, I did it!

I found a Rashi that refers to this idea, in Bamidbor, an eye-opener, which explains exactly what the Rebbe did. Numbers 3,16. "Moshe counted them, by the mouth of G-d, as he had been commanded."

Rashi comments, "Moshe asked, 'How can I enter into a tent to know how many suckling babies there are?' The Holy One Blessed Be He said, 'You do what's upon you and I will do what's upon me.' Moshe stood on the threshold, and an echo of the Divine Presence told him the number of children in the tent."

That's what the Rebbe did. He stood on the doorsteps of universities, without knowing that anyone will come out from there. G-d said, "You do your part, I will do mine."

CD *One final question. After knowing the Rebbe for so many*

*years, would you consider yourself today a "hidden Chasid" or
even an "open Chasid"?*

DH   As I told you before, I lack something in being a Chasid. A
Chasid doesn't dare, it wouldn't be right for him, to ask the Rebbe
to explain this or that. That's my understanding of a Chasid. If I had
been that kind of a Chasid I would have stayed with my Litvische
Gaon and not gone any further. I might never have gotten involved
with the Rebbe. After all, I could have said to myself, "Look, this
man is an authority."

7

Dr. Norman Lamm

President, Yeshiva University, Rabbi and Author

TORAH UMADA

CD   *Rabbi Lamm, as the president of Yeshiva University for the last twenty years, I'd like to hear from you your impressions about the Rebbe and Lubavitch. I have heard that you had an interesting meeting with the Rebbe in Yechidus.*

NL   Before I tell you about the particular Yechidus, let me say from the outset that I am not a Lubavitcher Chasid; however, in general I am very kindly disposed to Chasidus, and I have a special respect and affection for Lubavitch. It does not mean that I am a Chasid, because if I were a Chasid I would accept everything the Rebbe said with no questions asked. It so happens that on almost all major policy decisions I would have disagreed with the decisions of the Rebbe. Yet I considered that he was preeminently the most distinguished, the most important Jewish manhig in my lifetime and probably in the last century, because his contribution to Yahadus was incalculable. I have a great, enormous respect for Lubavitch, not only the late Rebbe, but for the Chasidim too. Their work in the Chabad houses, in every area has been enormous.

I appreciate their openness. Whenever I travel out of the city, I come to a Bais Chabad or a Lubavitcher shul, your people are doing exactly what we did. In other words, in an attempt to reach the people, you don't throw every stringency at them. If you have to read a passage with them in English, you read it in English. If they come by car, you don't ask them any questions because they're going to ride anyway. You don't make it a policy you're allowed to ride with a car, but you don't make a policy that if you ride with a car you can't come into my shul. This has basically been our approach all along. Until you have enough people to set up in a community by your standards. I think it's intelligent. It's the way things should be done.

Getting back to the Yechidus, it was probably in 1956 that I met the Rebbe of blessed memory. It was about the day school we had in Springfield Mass., where I was a Rabbi. We had a day school and there was also a Lubavitcher day school. My concern was that there was competition for a very few students. I came to the Rebbe. I saw him quite late at night, I don't remember exactly what time. He took a halachic stance, that there is no Hasogas Gevul, no encroachment when it comes to disseminating the Torah. That's the way it remained. He didn't order any change. To this day there are two schools that operate separately. I was not necessarily pleased with this decision but I respected it.

CD *You were the principal of the other school?*

NL I wasn't the principal — I was a rabbi in the community. I felt responsible for that day school because it was the day school that serviced my congregation. Like so many suburban or out of New York day schools, it had quite a number of non-orthodox kids from non-orthodox families whom we tried to bring closer to YIddishkeit. The same was true of the Lubavitcher day school.

I had tried to effect some sort of unification but it didn't work. I accepted the Rebbe's decision, and never held it against him or the Lubavitcher in Springfield, who are still very dear friends, people I like very much, like the Eidelman's.

CD *Were there any personal or philosophical things discussed during the Yechidus?*

NL No.

CD *Were you here in America when the Previous Rebbe came in*

1940?

NL   I was a Bar-Mitzvah boy at the time. I was born here. I must tell you that to my recollection, the impact that the Previous Rebbe had was nowhere near as widespread and powerful as the last Rebbe. There were a number of Chasidishe Rebbeim. All of them had a certain amount of prominence, but no one really overwhelmed the public. It's the most recent Lubavitcher Rebbe who had this tremendously wide influence and broad impact on the Jewish community as a whole.

CD   *Can you tell me about your philosophical approach to Torah Umada? I have read your book,* Torah Umada, *and see several ideas that resemble concepts mentioned in Chasidus.*

NL   My view of Torah Umada is based largely on a Chasidic concept, the idea of Avodah B'Gashmius. As I write in my book, the Chasidic Gedolim themselves did not approve of science in their generations, but, nevertheless, it follows logically from their premises. I think the Lubavitcher are probably the closest to us in that respect. The Rebbe himself did not forswear advanced secular education. He himself studied in Berlin and at the Sorbonne, and he sent his talmidim here. We have a number of talmidim who were sent here by the Rebbe.

    If he really thought they should not be exposed to Torah Umada he wouldn't have let them come within a mile of us. To wit, certain Litvishe Yeshivas. The Rebbe on the contrary — we never considered him anything but a close friend.

CD   *You studied with Rabbi Soloveitchik?*

NL   Of course.

CD   *Did you ever hear from Rabbi Soloveitchik discussions about the Rebbe?*

NL   No. He may have had them, but I didn't hear. I certainly never heard any criticism. I know that later on he went into Crown Heights for a farbrengen. I think he was there also for the Shiva call. It is obvious that he would not have gone had he not had a lot of respect for him. The Rov did not go to other people just like this. He had a lot of respect, I know, for Reb Aron Kotler of blessed memory, and for the Lubavitcher Rebbe. To say that there was any kind of split between them would have been terribly wrong. On the contrary.

CD   *I also understand from some of your writings that you have a specific point of view on Orthodoxy. What is your understanding of what the Rebbe has done for Orthodoxy?*

NL   The Rebbe did an enormous amount for Orthodoxy. The idea of kiruv that was accomplished by Lubavitch is incredible. I think we were "the first kids on the block" when it came to that. I remember in the 1950's we had these huge seminars that our Yeshiva founded. Later, because of financial reasons, we had to pull back and others came to fill the void, but Lubavitch acted on its own, separately from some of the others. They have done tremendous good. I applaud them.

CD   *What is your position on the upcoming elections in Eretz Yisroel?*

NL   I wouldn't go into that because it is a political discussion, which is more nuanced than you want to hear. I'm not a dove and I'm not a hawk. I feel that a lot of the talk is overblown. We are right before the elections, and we're not getting an honest opinion by anyone, either by Labor or Likud. I think that whoever wins is going to have to do more or less the same thing. The difference will be only in style, not in substance. I'm not terribly excited about this election, one way or the other. What concerns me in the long run, more than the peace process, is the Kulturkampf that's taking place. That bothers me. Here I feel that the real issue is, are we going to be a nation like all the nations, or are we going to be an Am Segulah? That is much more critical for the future development of

Am Yisroel and Medinas Yisroel than whether we are going to negotiate with the Arabs with a smile or with a smirk.

CD   *Have you yourself attended a farbrengen?*

NL   No. I've seen it on television but I haven't been there.

CD   *I detect in your writing Chasidus. Have you actually learned Tanya?*

NL   Well, I come from a Chasidic background somewhat. My grandfather of blessed memory Harav Yehoshuah Baumol was a very, very prominent Williamsburg Rav, the author of Teshuvah Seforim which dealt with some of the most important halachic problems of World War Two and that period. He himself was not a Rebbe by any means, but he was the first Rosh Yeshiva in Vishnitz when he was 16 or 17 years old. He started the Vishnitzer Yeshiva in Vishnitz. He came from that lineage, from the Tzanzer background.

My other grandfather of blessed memory was a simple person. He was not a Rov, but he was a man who traveled to the Belzer Rov in Lemberg. So I come from Chasidic background and therefore feel very close. What happened was, when I was in college I used to read on my own the history of Chasidus, because of my family interest, and then, after I got Semichah and I decided to go for a doctorate, I did my work on Reb Chaim Volozhiner, which led me of course to Lubavitch and in turn to Tanya. I learned Tanya and Likutei Torah in an attempt to understand the differences between Chasidus and Hisnagdus. You have that in my Sefer on Torah Lishmoh. It is really a story of the growth of Hisnagdus and the relationship between Hisnagdus and Chasidus.

That sefer was printed originally in Hebrew by Mosad Harav Kook, and subsequently came out in an English translation called "Torah For Torah's Sake" published by Ktav. I can give you a copy if you wish. It constantly refers to Chabad, because Chabad obviously has the most articulate exposition of Chasidus. Almost all the others are Droshos, a good Vort which was said at Sholosh

94

Seudos, which a Chasid recorded. But the leaders of the Chabad movement, they themselves wrote. They wrote seforim directly on Machshovoh, Jewish thought and Divrei Elokim Chaim, (Kabbalah and Chasidus). So here you have it straight, and it is much more systematic, much more organized.

CD   *In your analysis of Reb Chaim Volozhiner, do you see a major philosophical difference that led to the split between the groups?*

NL   I see a major philosophical difference between the Chasidim and Misnagdim as represented by the difference between Reb Chaim as a talmid of the Vilna Gaon and the Baal haTanya as a talmid of the Magid. The differences are very subtle. Major consequences to the differences, but the differences themselves are very subtle and they go within the same context. It's not as if one is coming from left field and one from right field. They are in the same context of how you interpret certain elements, in the detail of dealing with the result of Tzimtzum, the contraction of G-d's infinite energy.

There, I think I've discovered the nub of the differences which leads one to transcendence or to immanence, and how they relate to each other. It leaves one with a great deal of respect for both sides.

CD   *I don't really understand the view of the Vilna Gaon, how Tzimtzum is to be understood in the simple sense. He seems to say that Hashem in His true essence left the universe!*

NL   This difference goes back even before the Gaon. I'll give you the sefer in English so that you can better understand where the Vilna Gaon was coming from.

CD   *I have seen some Rabbinic graduates of Yeshiva University who have become Conservative rabbis. Is my assumption wrong? I'm not saying it's rampant. However, why is it?*

NL   It's a generational thing. This happened, for instance, when I graduated from Yeshiva College in 1949, there were still people, generally on the lowest level of the class, who thought they couldn't hack it here, couldn't make it, couldn't go into a semicha program that had a Rav Soloveitchik , and they also probably were more economically oriented, so they went to the Conservative movements seminary. This wasn't only here. I could show you now leading reform and conservative rabbis who come from Torah Vodaas and Chaim Berlin. We always produced more rabbonim, so with us it was more emphatic. I am here president almost twenty years. I don't know of a single student who went to the Seminary during these last twenty years. I could show you a number of students who came from the Seminary to us. The wheel turns over. It's a completely different orientation.

       Now we have people coming to us from the outside in general. Completely from secular backgrounds. Coming to learn, and many of them become Rabbonim and Rosh Yesivos. Not merely musmochim in pulpits, but Rosh Yeshivos, and some of the finest. So we have people who defected to the conservative movement a generation or two ago. Now we have people who have defected in the other direction, ones who used to be anti-yeshiva becoming pro-yeshiva, generally associating with the Litvishe yeshivos, but we haven't had any defections to the left in at least twenty years. A whole different atmosphere.

CD   *Would you say that the initiation of the Torah Umada movement would be with the Vilna Gaon's allowing of certain ideologies that were not in the Jewish community at that moment?*

NL   What kind of ideologies did he allow?

CD   *When the Haskalah movement came to Russia from Germany, and they began to emphasize teaching Dikduk, Hebrew grammar. I have also read that the Vilna Gaon sent some of the Talmidim to study general secular studies.*

NL   It's true and it's not true. See, the idea of emphasizing Hebrew grammar comes much before the influence of the Haskalah. It goes back to the Maharal. So does the emphasis on Machshovoh. It goes back to the Maharal, who was really a first-rate educational reformer who was critical of the extant system.

Incidentally, we have now reverted to the system that he criticized. We teach Gemorah and that's all; you start a boy on Gemorah before he knows how to read Chumash and Rashi, and you put him into pilpul immediately. The Maharal was very upset by it. He was a great educational reformer; that tendency was there already.

What the Gaon did was not to battle the Haskalah, which I don't think affected him very much directly. It was a generation later that that took place. What he did was, he told his talmidim, that there should be some understanding of mathematics, and there-fore Reb Boruch Mishklov writes in the introduction to one of his seforim that the Gaon asked him to translate Euclid from Greek into Hebrew and also told him the famous statement that certain people say is not authentic, but that itself is propaganda. It's authentic; I'm 100% sure it's authentic. "When a person lacks one measure of the world's wisdom, there are 10 measures of Torah wisdom that are lacking." That is very important for our Hashkafah, philosophical view.

Torah Umada draws in this sense to some extent on the Misnagdic groups and to some extent on the chasidic groups. It's simply an attempt to find, from within our own tradition, the abili-ty to approach the world in this particular way.

The Gaon was attempting to bring legitimate Chochmas Haolom, worldly knowledge, into the Jewish community, and he had some talmidim, such as Reb Menashe of Ilya who were very important in setting up a different kind of educational system, one which would prepare students more rationally, more intelligently for being able to understand Tanach and Torah Sheb'al Peh, the Oral Torah.

I don't think they were very successful. And I think the rea-son they weren't very successful was because the Haskalah came along and radicalized the frum community. If not for the Haskalah,

I think naturally the frum community would have come to the same conclusion in a context of Emunah. Once they had to fight the Haskalah, with its excesses, it no longer followed what I would call a natural development, which would have had Limudei Chol in the context of Yiras Shomayim. That threw a crimp into the whole development.

CD   *Thank you for your time. Let us meet in Yerusholayim, together with Moshiach.*

8

Mr. Nathan Lewin

Attorney, Washington, D.C., President of Jewish Lawyers and Jurists, Vice President COLPA

JUDAISM'S LAWYER

CD   *Please tell me a little about yourself.*

NL   I am a resident of Washington DC. I was born in Poland, in Lodz. My grandfather, Zal, was the Raisha Rov, very important in Galicia. He was in the Polish Parliament, leader of the community in Poland, and I'm told a great orator and speaker in Polish, a leader of Agudas Yisroel. His grandfather was the Bais Yitzchok, R Yitzchok Shmelkes, whom you certainly may know of, a Posek and Av Beis Din in Lemberg, and may father of blessed memory was Dr. Yitzchok Levine, who was a leader in the Agudah here in the U.S.. He left Europe in 1939 and came here early 1941. My father was active in Kahal matters, in addition to being a professor of Jewish history in Yeshivah University and other jobs. He was very active in terms of Hatzolah matters during the war. He himself had various contacts with the Rebbe over the years, has some letters from the Rebbe about the activities he engaged in.

I am a lawyer in Washington. I have been active since I left the government. I learned at Yeshiva University, R. Yitzchok Elchonan, went to Harvard Law School, and clerked for the US court of appeals for the second circuit and then for the supreme court of the US, for Justice John Holme, and then was in the government for a number of years. I argued cases in the Supreme Court and then left for private practice in 1969, and have been active, since I began private practice, on all different kinds of issues of

Jewish concern in the courts. I have had the privilege of presenting a number of important Jewish questions in the Supreme Court of the United States, questions of Sabbath observance. Afterwards I drafted the law that protects Sabbath observers in private employment. I have litigated that in courts, I argued that in the Supreme Court of the United States, argued the case of the right to wear a Yarmulke in the military...

CD   *Goldman?*

NL   The Goldman case. I've argued on behalf of both Satmar and Lubavitch. I represented Satmar in the Kiryas Joel case in Supreme Court and also in a redistricting case a number of years ago in a Jewish organization in Williamsburg, which was about redistricting in the Satmar community. I've represented Lubavitch in the Supreme court about the right to put up a Menorah in a public place, in front of the Pittsburgh city hall, which we won in the Supreme court, and now, in lower courts of appeals, and, as a matter of fact, we won yesterday in the court of appeals for southern circuit of the Federal Court in Chicago. In Atlanta, in Grand Rapids, Michigan, in Cincinnati, Ohio, in various locations around the country, I have fought for this right, in most cases on behalf of local Chabad groups.

CD   *You're the president of COLPA [National Jewish Commission on Law and Public Affairs, a volunteer group of attorneys and social scientists who advocate for Orthodox causes]?*

NL   I've been ever since it was formed. It was formed when I was still in the government. I've avoided being president just because I dislike administrative and fundraising things, but I have been its vice president ever since 1969, when I went out private practice. I do almost all its briefs and I've been president of the Jewish Community Council of Greater Washington, president of an organization known as the international association of Jewish lawyers and Jurists, which is an international Jewish lawyers' group, whose activities don't involve fundraising.

CD   *How did your involvement with the seforim, with the books in the Rebbe's library, begin?*

NL   My recollection was the first I heard of it being called for advice by Rabbi Krinsky,who I think was acting at the suggestion of the Rebbe. I received a call in which I was told that they had discovered that someone was removing books from the storage place where there was the library of the previous Rebbe. The question was, what was the proper course, could or should there be a criminal challenge made, things of that type.

My understanding was that this had been discovered by the installation of video surveillance equipment and that prior to that time, the reason that there had been a belief that books had been removed was that some of the seforim had shown up on the international antiques market in Judaica, in Europe and in Israel. Rabbi Krinsky called me late at night, I recall. I had fallen asleep and he called me that he had this information, the question was what to do, and he told me that it was unfortunately the nephew of the Rebbe who they had seen on the surveillance camera, taking the seforim. I said at that the time that it seemed to me he was probably going to make some claim of ownership to them and that therefore it was probably not desirable to make this a criminal charge.

I think the next day or two days later Rabbi Krinsky came down to Washington to my office to discuss what to do about this. He was the only client I've had who brought with him a page of the Choshen Mishpat specifically on the matter of going to civil court in a matter between Jewish people. We discussed the question of why it was necessary maybe to go to court rather than go to a Bais Din, based on the simple question that the books were in the process of being sold. We knew that the books were being sold, and offered by dealers, and a list had apparently been prepared by a dealer who was able to offer some of the books. I told Rabbi Krinsky it was possible to go to court simply to get a restraining order that would keep the person that had the books from disposing of them until there could be a Din Torah. It was on that basis, after he went back, that he called and said we should prepare the papers.

We checked and discovered that Barry Gurary was a resident of New Jersey, and that made it possible for us to sue in federal court, which was better than suing in state court in New York.

We prepared the papers in order to serve him in federal court. We had this information about the books being sold abroad in the antiques market . On that basis we prepared the papers and went ahead. At some point, also, prior to the time that the papers were filed, Rabbi Krinsky and Rabbi Shemtov introduced me also to Joe Shestack, of Philadelphia, whom I may have met at some point previous but did not know that well. He was also involved in the filing of the papers.

CD   *You mentioned that Rabbi Krinsky brought you the page from Choshen Mishpat. Was that to show that you didn't have to go to a Bais Din?*

NL   Yes. Because the Bais Din could not provide the relief that we needed at that point., If we went to Bais Din then he would go out immediately and try to dispose of all the remaining books. The Bais Din would not be able to issue any effective restraining order against him. Whereas a court order that would be enforceable by contempt would be able to prevent the books from being sold. We decided to do it sort of as a surprise.

We would go into court, serve him with the papers immediately so he would not be able to sell books in the meantime, and get a temporary restraining order from the court so that immediately he would be prevented from selling any books under pain of contempt. We would be sure that no more books would be sold. It had already been decided that the books that had been sold would be bought back, the process may have already begun. The purpose of bringing the page of Choshen Mishpot — not to prove it to me, he was coming with the authority of the Rebbe — nonetheless to make sure that I understood that the question of going to Bais Din had been thoroughly considered. This was for a limited purpose — our original complaint only asked for a restraining order so the books could not be sold.

CD   *The halacha provides this heter?*

NL   Yes, that was the point. If you cannot get from Bais Din what you can get from arko'os, for that limited purpose you can go to arko'os. Then we filed the papers. The way it works is you draw a judge. As soon as you file the papers the court spins a wheel and pulls out the name of a judge. The judge was Judge Sifton, whom I had not appeared before previously, but who was a respected judge. It turned out his first wife was the daughter of Reinhold Niebuhr, who was a famous Christian theologian, and that added to his interest in the case. We would have to go immediately to a Judge to get this temporary restraining order signed, and what happened is, Judge Sifton goes on vacation. The judge assigned with emergency matters was a Judge Glasser, a Jewish judge. We went into chambers. Just before I filed the papers, I had notified Barry Gurary, so we could get this temporary restraining order. His lawyer was Al Hellerstein.

      We went to Judge Glasser. I remember noticing the judge was Jewish enough that he had framed on his wall the front page from an early edition of the Rambam. We sat down, and the judge said, "This looks to me like the kind of case that ought to go to a Rabbinic Court." We had just brought this suit against Barry Gurary saying that these books were the property of the community, of the Agudas Chasidei Chabad. We said, "If we get an order that he can't sell the books, we are prepared to go to a Rabbinic court for the rest of the case.

      Mr. Hellerstein said on behalf of Barry Gurary, "Now that we're in court, we confess that we are going to challenge the ownership of this library, and we are going to do this in court here, so we are not prepared to go to a Rabbinic Court." On that basis the judge said OK. He signed the restraining order, which kept him from selling the books, and also signed an order which required him to give us a list of all the books that he had. It turned out that he had gone through the library catalogue on a computer and had pulled out some of the most valuable books, incunabula, books that were printed before 1500, some manuscripts. In fact, one manuscript had already been sold for $25,000 or so. We got that list.

CD   *He went through the computer in the library?*

NL   No, apparently after he had carried out the books, he put it on a computer for purposes of the dealers that he was selling it to, a list of all the books. That list he was forced to give us by court order.

CD   *How did he get in?*

NL   I understood he got in because his mother gave him the key. In fact, his mother joined the lawsuit on his side. Before the lawsuit we discussed what his mother's position was going to be, and we didn't know. But soon after we brought the lawsuit, his mother also, through Mr. Hellerstein, entered an appearance issue to intervene on his side. Her claim was that the library belonged to the family, to her and to her sister, and that was it. It was their library, therefore they could do with it as they wished, and she had given Barry permission to take out whatever books he wanted, and her sister, according to her, had agreed, and on that basis he took out these books. Of course, our position was that they were not the family's books, they were the community's books, and they belonged to Agudas Chasidei Chabad.

    That gave us an indication of where she was. There was also some question about where the librarian might be in the lawsuit. He ended up siding with Barry Gurary and his mother, claiming this was a family library. That was how the case began. Over the succeeding months, when we had the order in effect, and some books were being bought back, of course the case was litigated, and ultimately there was a trial before a judge, which was an enormously interesting trial. I can tell you, it was the best-attended trial I have ever appeared in. Every seat was taken in every session. Buses came in from Crown Heights, full of people who wanted to watch the trial. It was also the best-fed case I've ever argued, because every day lunch was brought from Crown Heights.

    It was very fortunate that the judge in the next courtroom was a judge who was not a hard worker, so he was very seldom in court. What we would do was at lunch time we would go to the next courtroom and spread out the lunch at the lawyers' table and eat, of course davven mincha after lunch.

CD *When did you first talk to the Rebbe about this?*

NL   We filed the case on the basis of my meetings and discussions with Rabbi Krinsky, and some other people. This was the temporary restraining order. After we had gotten the temporary restraining order and Barry's mother had become a party to the case, Rabbi Krinsky advised me that the Rebbe wanted to meet with Mr. Shestack and myself, so I came up and we had a meeting with the Rebbe which lasted about an hour, to discuss the case, what the positions were of the parties, and what positions witnesses should take, who was likely to be called as witnesses.

CD *Were you giving the Rebbe the information or was he giving you the information?*

NL   We were giving the information on where the case stood, although it was clear to us from the meeting that the Rebbe had been reading all the pleadings, and was fully familiar with where the case stood, although we gave him our impressions and evaluations of what was likely to happen and how the process worked. He giving us the view of how the case should be addressed. An initial position that the Rebbe felt very strongly, which made very good sense to me, although judge did not accept it as a means of finishing the case at the outset, was that whatever one said about who owned the books, Barry Gurary did not do it in a way that was appropriate for someone who owned it — he went in the middle of the night and he took it, it was a gnaiva — therefore, at the very least, the books should be put back, and then if he disagrees, let him bring a case. We did take that argument and tried to present it to judge as a basis for terminating the case at that point, but the court did not accept that.

CD *Your argument, based on the Rebbe's argument was, "If it's his, why did he steal it?"*

NL   Right.

CD   *Why did the judge reject that argument?*

NL   He said that the whole issue of ownership had been raised in the case, and he was going to decide the issue of ownership. Look, I think the Rebbe was clearly right! He should put the books back, and then if he has a complaint let him bring a lawsuit, but in the meantime the books should be brought back to where they were! He had no business taking them in the middle of the night even if he had some basis for thinking they were his. Both Shestack and I agreed with that position, but the judge did not accept that.

That was the subject of the first meeting with the Rebbe, as well as the whole question, also at the second meeting. We had a long second meeting after this initial stage in which the progress of the case was discussed, and the question of who would be the witnesses. At that point they had indicated that they wanted to take the deposition of the Rebbitzen, which they ultimately took.

They also made claim that they wanted to take the deposition of the Rebbe. We thought that was inappropriate — there was nothing the Rebbe could say, and the Rebbe also felt that that was not something that should be done, there was no particular evidence that he had with respect to it, and it was just not appropriate that the Rebbe be deposed. We were successful in preventing a deposition after that initial threat.

CD   *At the farbrengen's where I was present, the Rebbe's voice was louder than usual and he had a lot to say about the issue!*

NL   A lot to say, but not direct evidence about who owned it, whereas the Rebbitzen could speak about her father, and what her father's intention would have been with respect to his library. The Rebbe had never had any discussion with the previous Rebbe about the ownership of that library, nothing that would be evidence in a court. He had his opinions, his opinions were stated in farbrengen's, but that was not evidence. The truth is the other side was trying to use that as a means of harassing us, because they knew it was not seemly, was not appropriate that they should do that. They were trying to use that as a tactical maneuver. I think ultimately that the court recognized that that was not appropriate, and we were successful in preventing it. Ultimately, for various reasons, they withdrew, they didn't push. I think Mr. Hellerstein recognized himself that that was not appropriate.

CD   *The Rebbitzen was deposed at her home?*

NL   Yes, there's a videotape of that. I have it at home.

CD   *What did she say?*

NL   She denied that she gave permission to her sister, and she said that the books were the property of the community.

CD   *In talking with the Rebbe, did he talk about the fact that his wife's sister was bringing the lawsuit?*

NL   No, not about personalities. The only thing that he did say was that Barry took the books without any permission. It was Agudas Chasidei Chabad who was bringing the lawsuit

CD   *Against Barry Gurary or his mother too?*

NL   By then his mother was in the lawsuit, so it was clear that she was also a party.

CD   *Was the Rebbe very aggravated, when you met him for the first time?*

NL   The impression was he was upset; however his tone was low-key. I understand that at the Farbrengen his voice was louder, but with us he was very, very calm about it and very much to the point about the case, discussing the different theories. At some point, I think it may even have been in the first meeting, he pointed up what ultimately ended up being the key piece of evidence, a letter that the previous Rebbe had written to professor Alexander Marx at the Jewish Theological Seminary. We discussed that letter, and how that letter said that the books were the property of the community and a treasure of the community. The Rebbe very strongly felt that that document showed that the Previous Rebbe had intended that this would be the property of Agudas Chasidei Chabad or the community, and not personal property of the family. That certainly ended up being the key piece of evidence.

In preparing the case, Rabbi Krinsky and a couple of the others, Rabbi Levin included, had put together some of the materials, including this letter to Marx, that would show that it was community property. The Rebbe spent some time discussing that letter and the ramifications of it and what it meant in terms of proving what the Previous Rebbe's intention was.

CD   *What did the letter actually say?*

NL   My recollection is it was to urge him to get the American government and everyone else to find that library and bring it over to the United States — this is at a time when it was still not known where the library was and if it could be brought here — and the statements in that letter were that this library is a treasure of the community, and things like that. That was the reason that he said to Marx that the efforts should be made to bring it over. Of course the other side said that he was saying it only for the purpose of getting Marx or the United States government interested in bringing the library over, that it was really the family's. That raises another question. We said that the Previous Rebbe would not have lied in a letter to Marx.

My recollection is that we did discuss that with the Rebbe too, and the Rebbe was upset at the notion that the claim was made that the previous Rebbe had lied. He said clearly he wouldn't lie for anything like this, you are not allowed to lie. We had a discussion in terms of sheker, that you can't lie, midvar sheker tirchak. I know this came out of the trial ultimately, this whole question of whether this statement made to Marx was a lie, and we said the Rebbe wouldn't lie. My recollection is that judge may even have referred to that in his opinion.

CD   *On your part there was no attempt to prevent the deposition of the Rebbitzen?*

NL   We may initially have raised some questions, but then they made a showing that she may have had some discussions about it. Then, of course, on the question of whether she had given permission, there was no question that she was a witness. There was no question that since Barry's mother said that the Rebbitzen had given permission, she was entitled to have the Rebbitzen's testimony on whether she had indeed given permission. The Rebbe denied that she had, but, at least on that matter, there was no way to avoid the deposition.

CD   *These seforim were the ones that were brought over from Poland? Rabbi Shemtov, I remember, years ago brought over a library of the Previous Rebbe's from Poland.*

NL   Yes, this was the library that the Previous Rebbe had collected after his initial library, which is still in Russia, the library we're trying to get out now, was taken by the Bolsheviks. Then he had his secretary, Lieberman, begin to collect a library which he wanted should match the greatest Jewish libraries in the world. They began collecting in the early 1920's and also asking people to send books, if they can, to the Lubavitcher Rebbe. Notices were given in Pardes and in other magazines and journals, to send copies [of seforim] to the Lubavitcher Rebbe and so on, and on that basis this library was collected. Then the war broke out.

The Rebbe went to Otwock. From Otwock I think there's another letter he wrote, to Agudas Chasidei Chabad in the US at that time, the only letter that came from the Rebbe describing that he is there, his plan of travel, but also pleading with them to please make sure that this library is packaged and brought to the United States because it is so important. There also are statements made that Agudas Chasidei Chabad in the United States should be the ones who have this library. The interesting thing in connection with this trial — I went back over the old records of the wartime period, both in 770 which Rabbi Krinsky had put together, and, in addition, I went back to the State Department documents and found there are some very interesting documents about how the Previous Rebbe had been brought out of Poland to the United States — it had been done through Agudas Chasidei Chabad.

One of our points was that Agudas Chasidei Chabad in the United States was very much responsible for bringing the Rebbe out — it was a connection from someone to Justice Brandeis, and from Justice Brandeis to Ben Cohen, and Ben Cohen to the secretary of state, Cordell Hull, and then they brought the Previous Rebbe out that way, by special request, to Germany, which was still a friend of the United States in 1940. That was how he and the whole group, Rabbi Gurary, Chanah, and Lieberman all came that way, first by train and by boat to Sweden, then from Sweden to the United States .

CD   *So what was the point of that argument?*

NL   The point of that argument was that from the time the library was created it was the property of the community, and even if it was not from the time it was created, the Rebbe made it the property of the community at some point. The judge did say that yes, the Rebbe did create a trust which he set up, holding it for the community. Our point was that he had reason to do that, because this was essentially the organization that rescued him from Europe. Essentially, he was saying, OK, you will be the repository of this library. He had a reason to do that, because they were the ones that were bringing the whole thing out.

CD   *The judge accepted that argument?*

NL   The judge accepted the argument that it was a trust for the community, that the Rebbe was holding it in trust for the community.

CD   *Even though, legally, it was not set up as a trust?*

NL   Right, because according to the law in the United States, you can create a trust even without legal documents. If you say, "I am the trustee of such-and-such," you immediately become the trustee. Of course, it's better if you have a legal document, you can create a trust for certain people, becomes the trustee of someone. That was his conclusion to this. The letter to Marx was evidence of the fact that he viewed this as a trust that he was holding it for Agudas Chasidei Chabad.

CD   *Did you have a third meeting with the Rebbe?*

NL   After the case was won, we had a very brief third session. Then I saw the Rebbe at different times, on Sundays.

CD   *The Rebbe didn't correspond in writing with you?*

NL   No, nothing in writing. Just two meetings, each about an hour, Jerry Shestack and myself. I remember, at the beginning of the first meeting we discussed what language he should speak, and I would have been comfortable in Yiddish but Jerry Shestack would not, so we spoke in English. The Rebbe asked whether we should speak in Yiddish or in French or in English.

CD   *Did they go to the court of appeals?*

NL   Yes, they appealed and lost.

CD   *The Menorah issue, did you ever discuss that with the Rebbe?*

NL   I discussed the menorah issue on one of the subsequent encounters on Sunday. I know this, because at one point I gave him a progress report on where we were. It was later, after we won in the Pittsburgh case, that we began to assert the right to put up a

Menorah in various other cities. On each occasion I would discuss these with Rabbi Krinsky, and he said to me that he had discussed them with the Rebbe. He was pleased with the progress of the cases, because they were all going very well.

CD   *It seems that the victory in Pittsburgh was very limiting; as I recall, it was "If there's a Xmas tree, there's a Menorah." Is that correct?*

NL   The ruling was, that as part of a display which included an Xmas tree, there could be a Menorah.

CD   *That's very limiting.*

NL   Sure. That was the original decision. On that basis we went out in cases where we had a Menorah separately, without a Xmas tree. The cases we won, including the case we just won in Indianapolis, involved a Menorah all by itself. Grand Rapids, also.

CD   *What was the logic? How did you get from "a" to "b"?*

NL   True, that case involved an overall change in approach , but we said, nonetheless, and indicated, that a Menorah was not a violation of the establishment clause. The next step is that putting up a Menorah in a public place is freedom of speech. This was the catch, with which we won a bunch of these cases, and the Supreme Court has now approved that in this case involving the Ku Klux Klan, which came in after us. That's the case just decided this past June, based on all the victories we had had. We made this point, that a Menorah is freedom of speech. If you put up a Menorah it's a religious display, but you're allowed to put up a religious display in a public forum, that is a place that's open to all kinds of other displays. You can't prevent us from putting up a Menorah in a public forum, and the courts accepted that. In Atlanta we got the right to put it up in the Rotunda of the state Capitol, all by itself, not with a Xmas tree, because it's freedom of speech.

CD   *That was a different argument from before?*

NL   Different than in Pittsburgh. In Pittsburgh it was the city's display. The question was, can the city put up a Menorah? The court said, in the context of the entire display, the Menorah is not a violation of the Establishment Clause. One thing I insisted on is that we say over and over again that the Menorah is a religious symbol. Lots of people have said, including the American Jewish Committee, that in order to win that case, Chabad persuaded the Supreme court that the Menorah is a secular symbol and not a religious symbol, and that's a lie.

The Supreme Court says 10 times in the decision that it's a religious symbol. There has never been a brief which I have filed on behalf of the Menorah in which I have not said that the Menorah is a religious symbol. The only case in which Chabad has said that the Menorah is not a religious symbol was in a case in California, before I represented Chabad, in which, I thought it was very unfortunate, some lawyer out there put in some affidavit saying that a Menorah is a secular symbol. Since I have represented Chabad we have never said that. We have always said that a Menorah is a religious symbol, but that we're entitled to put up a religious symbol in those places.

The Supreme Court in the Pittsburgh case said yes, the Menorah is a religious symbol, but in the context of the overall display, with a Xmas tree that's three times the size the Xmas tree outranks the Menorah. The Xmas tree was 48 foot high, the Menorah was 15 feet high, I think. I put a picture of those 2 things, one next to the other, into the Supreme Court brief, in order to show how crazy it is to say the city of Pittsburgh is encouraging Chanukah or being Jewish, when it's next to a Xmas tree that's three times the size.

So we won that case because a religious symbol like a Menorah could be put up by the city of Pittsburgh as part of an overall display. Then we went on in other cases to say the religious display is freedom of speech. I have the right to put up a religious display in a public forum. If I can put up a sign about AIDS, or I can put up a sign about abortion, or about the war in Bosnia, I can put up a sign about religion too. The courts have agreed with that proposition — you're allowed to put up a religious symbol in a public place.

CD   *What about a separation?*

NL   Separation has nothing to do with private speech. The government can't engage in religion. My point of view always is, in this case and the others, private exercise of religion is protected by the Constitution, and we should be able to engage in that fully. Private exercise of religion. I'm not in favor of the government writing a prayer, and forcing people to say the government's prayer — but I am in favor of people being allowed to pray privately wherever — public schools, public places. Private prayer should be permitted.

CD   *And they accepted it.*

NL   They accepted it. Based on that, the Ku Klux Klan got the right to put up a cross. And based on the Ku Klux Klan's getting the right to put up a cross, the court of appeals in Chicago has now ruled that we have the right to put up a Menorah.

CD   *To sum it up, what are your impressions of the Rebbe?*

NL   It was obviously a very moving, impressive experience to be discussing any matter with the Rebbe. He was very astute with respect to how the case was proceeding and how it should proceed, it was all in all a very principled discussion, discussing the principle of the case and how we should be able to present it to the court, to make them understand the Rebbe's position. As we see from the opinion, we see the Marx letter, which the Rebbe had emphasized, was the key document for Judge Sifton. I've been asked about the Rebbe many times by people all over the world — I still remember years ago, I went to Leningrad, and I went to the shul where Chabad had its Yeshiva, and they were learning. This was when Glasnost was first beginning. In Gorbachev's days it was still very difficult to bring in books and other things like that. We met many Jews in Leningrad, and most were thinking of going on Aliyah, they would have practical questions, getting a job, and so on .We went to a Chasunah, a couple of Baalei Teshuvah in Leningrad who were getting married — a triple Chasunah, as I remember.

One young man who was learning at the Yeshiva had been introduced to me as an genius. At this Chasunah he came over to me and said, "You know, if you have a few minutes could I please speak to you?" I said OK, I was sure he would speak to me about Eretz Yisroel, what's going to be. We went over to the other room and we were all by ourselves, he says to me , "I understand you had a meeting with the Rebbe — could you just tell me exactly what the Rebbe said to you and what you said to the Rebbe?" That's all that he wanted to know.

CD   *Once you spoke in "770" and you mentioned that your grandfather had a connection to the previous Rebbe?*

My father had, and my brother also has had. My father had a whole thing with a book. He has published a number of books of essays, Jewish history matters. He taught the history of the Jews in Poland in Yeshiva University, also he was an expert in Responsa on Jewish topics, and things like that. He published a number of books in Hebrew and English and Polish and Yiddish. One of the seforim that he sent to the Rebbe, (he would regularly send his books to the Rebbe and get letters back as a response) the Rebbe wrote him back and said that it was very good, but it seems that the last essay had been on a somewhat discouraging note, and he should end with a more positive note. In the second edition, he incorporated the Rebbe's suggestion and concluded his last essay on a positive note.

9

Rabbi Nissen Mangel

Author, Translator, Professor Beth Rivka Seminary,
Worldwide Lecturer on Jewish Mysticism

HOLOCAUST TO MOSHIACH'S ARRIVAL

CD   *Please begin with your background, some details about being a holocaust survivor from Czechoslovakia.*

NM   I was born in a frum, observant, home. At the beginning of 1941 Hitler entered Czechoslovakia, gave a big chunk of Czechoslovakia to Hungary, made it into three parts. One part he annexed to Germany, the Sudeten, the Czech Republic became a puppet state under the dominion of Hitler, like the satellites of Russia. Slovakia became a puppet state, an independent Slovak republic. The Prime Minister and the President were vicious anti-Semites, both were priests of the Catholic Church.

This was the only country in the whole of Europe—this is not so well-known, but I think it should be publicized, that not only did he allow Jews to be taken to Auschwitz, but actually paid a head tax for each Jew that was taken to a concentration camp. What's so unique about this—everyone asks the question, "Where was the Pope?" And they answer that he was really friendly, just that he did not want to jeopardize the Catholic Church in Germany. But in Slovakia there was no excuse; The President and the Prime Minister both were princes of the Catholic Church, so there he certainly had an influence. It wasn't a question of a secular government. The secular government was run by priests. At the very least he could have admonished them, which he never did, threaten to excommunicate them, which he never did. And there would be no danger that the government would persecute Catholics, because the Prime Minister was a Catholic member of the clergy. Here we see clearly that the Church, to a certain extent, were collaborators with Hitler. Also, they took one part of Czechoslovakia and they gave it as a gift to Hitler, adding it to Hitler's hit list.

This city in which we were living, which was always part of Czechoslovakia, it became part of Hungary. Everyone's business was taken away. Only from the savings which we had could we live. When Hitler marched in, my father was a few weeks in Prague trying to get a visa to escape. All doors were closed. Eretz Yisroel, England, the United States. Panama was the only country that wanted to give us a visa. The day my father had gotten a visa from Panama, Hitler marched in to Prague. Finished. No one could get out, Jews included.

Then he divided Czechoslovakia. Our city went to Hungary. They decided that the Jews were not citizens, Jew who were born in Hungary. My grandparents were from Poland and came to Kosice, which was then in Czechoslovakia. My father was born in Kosice in 1902. They must have come at least five or ten years earlier.

In 1941 there came from Hungary over 80,000 Jews of Polish extraction. Living for a half century in this city, and they deported them. Over 85,000 Jews were killed at Babi Yar, Hungarian Jews, really Polish Jews, but Hungary never recognized them as citizens.

When this was going on, imagine only the persecutions which the Jews had to endure when Kosice became part of Hungary. In 1941 they didn't take Jews to Auschwitz. Only Jews who were born in Kosice — all other cities not. In 1941 they only took Poles who were not citizens, a non-citizen being someone who was not born in the country. In Slovakia they decided to take them only in 1942 to Auschwitz, regardless of whether they were citizens. This is anti-Semitism. You are foreigners! Ay, you lived for half a century or more than half a century, but you never obtained citizenship. And why didn't you obtain citizenship? Because they didn't want to give you! At least they had such an excuse. It's not that they didn't have this excuse. They took everybody in 1942. But they paid that Hitler should take them. It is unbelievable. It's not exposed. It happened specifically there, where the rulers of a secular government were priests.

Since my parents came from Slovakia, it is only because of Hitler that we were separated. My mother's whole family was in Slovakia. In 1942 when they started taking the Jews, they smuggled from the border children, from my uncles, and they were living with us, because children were very difficult to hide. We obtained VIP certificates that we are necessary for the government. We had to put up six of my cousins, children of my uncle.

It came 1944. By that time Slovakia was already "Juden rein" except these few Jews who had this VIP certificate, that they were necessary for the economy of the country and could stay. 300,000 Jews of Slovakia were killed at Auschwitz. Those who remained, remained, almost legally, because they had this certificate. This began in 1944. Thousands of Jews from Hungary were deported to Auschwitz.

The Germans occupied Hungary. So what did we do? We sent back the children over the border, that they should go back to their parents. They were caught. Here again a gantze maaseh. Can you imagine them being caught at the border? Anyway, at the beginning of April, or even earlier, in March, they marched through Hungary. Before that Hungary had been wavering. When it became clear that Germany was going to lose, they decided to be more independent, if not on the side of the allies, at least to separate themselves. When Hitler saw this he occupied Hungary, and began sending Jews to Auschwitz. The general who occupied Kosice came to the Jewish community and said that if they would give him a million dollars he wouldn't send them to Auschwitz. Do you know what $1,000,000 was then, in 1944? First of all, where do you get dollars? And the value of a dollar, more than 35 million dollars now, without any doubt, even more so. That Jews under German occupation should have one million dollars. Go back 5 years ago and look at the value of the dollar. Go back 40, 50 years ago.

Kosice had 30,000 Jews—a million dollars?

Anyway, everyone had to give. And if you couldn't give

how much you were taxed, they would come and say, give your beautiful Shabbos candlestick holders, give your Menorah, no one could escape. My family was well off, so they gave, and within 2 or 3 days a million dollars was raised with the hope that we wouldn't go to Auschwitz. As soon as they got the million dollars they started taking the Jews to Auschwitz. Deceitful.

CD   *How did you get out?*

NM   In short, I was in 6 different camps, death camps, and as the Chazal tell us, the word Nes has a nun, and the word Nissan has 2 nun's, Nisei Nisim. Miracles day in and day out.

I came back, my father didn't come back. From Auschwitz he was sent to Germany, and there, a group of friends were in the camp, four from Czechoslovakia, all Polish. They heard the Russians approaching Germany, the shooting of the guns and the artillery. Suddenly the SS decided to move them. They decided, why should they go further. One of the fellows decided to make a break. So he said to my father, "Come with me." In a few hours, maybe a day, we'll be freed! Why should we go further in another camp with the SS." This fellow said, "No, I cannot go alone, come with me." He says to my father, "Laizer, oh vay, du lust mir iber?", are you leaving me on my own. My father agreed to accompany him. As they walked out the SS saw them. As the Russians were coming on so fast, they couldn't evacuate them to another place in Germany, so they were shot on the spot. My father had Mesiras Nefesh for Ahavas Yisroel, to help this person.

The last camp, that I was sent to was in Guenstgueshen, Austria which is not very far from Linz, the second largest city in Austria. In Guenstgueshen I experienced Hashem's miracles. There I was with another person, he got typhus, was in delirium. Eventually we went to Linz. From Linz the Americans took us across the border to Czechoslovakia. All the cities were destroyed. Finally we arrived in Budapest. Eventually I came back to Czechoslovakia, to Kosice. I arrived Thursday night. We had our own house. I thought if I go home I won't find anybody. The Joint Distribution Committee had a hotel for homeless refugees in transit. I thought I would go to his hotel and see the next morning what would be. I came to our house 8 o'clock. I was afraid to go up, afraid I would see nobody in the house and have a nervous breakdown. I walked back and forth, back and forth. Eventually the building manager came out and I asked him if anyone of my family lived in my apartment. He said yes, your aunt is upstairs. Then I went up. I had a German uniform, an SS uniform. That's what I was wearing, an SS uniform. I came upstairs, I was emaciated, I didn't have any food for a long time. I looked terrible. When I opened the door my aunt screamed to her husband, " A tzigainer!," a thief is here to steal.

Initially they didn't recognize me. I said, "It's me!" They said my sister was also here, but she had a problem with her feet, and she was with a different relative. I was there for 3 or 4 weeks, and then we got a telegram from Prague that my mother had arrived. She is in Prague, she's coming. My mother, my sister, myself, that's all. We started life all over again. My mother opened up the store they owned before the war, and things actually went very well. Then in 1948, when the communists took over, we were afraid it would be just like Russia. They allowed children to go out, so with the hope that we would make it, first we went to Canada, and from Canada I went to England.

CD   *To Gateshead yeshiva?*

NM   No, to Sunderland, a small Yeshiva. There I learned from 1948 to 1951. Then I came back to Canada. I went to Lubavitcher Yeshiva in Montreal, it was almost the only Yeshiva. So I entered the world of Lubavitch and the rest is history.

CD   *I'd like to now turn to your first contact with the Rebbe. Had you written to the Rebbe ?*

NM   I was learning in Yeshiva, and it was over a year that I didn't get a visa to the US. I was not a citizen of anyplace. After the war you got a sort of passport, that your status was "stateless" . A year later I arrived in Montreal 1951, a year after the Rebbe accepted the leadership. In 1953 I obtained a visa. I came to New York for the Farbrengen of 12 Tammuz. Remember it was very small, just a little courtyard. I was standing near Binyomin Althaus. The Rebbe asked him, "Who is this bochur?" He said, "This is Nissan Mangel from Montreal." So immediately the Rebbe gave me some cake from his platter. This was the first Boruch Haba, welcome. I had not written to the Rebbe but I would imagine that someone would have let him know that I am coming. So when the Rebbe heard this is Nissan Mangel, he immediately gave me a big piece of cake.

The Rebbe said to me that on the way back to Montreal I should stop in a couple of places and speak words of Chasidus. I think I stopped in Albany and Buffalo. The Rebbe asked me whether I go every Shabbos to Shuls to chazer Chasidus. I said to the Rebbe, nobody does. So the Rebbe said, if you could pick up a thousand dollars, and nobody was picking it up would you refuse to pick it up because nobody was picking it up? Nobody goes! Then I found out the Rebbe wrote a letter to Rabbi Greenglass, the Mashpia, spiritual guide in the Yeshiva, that he heard from me that the bochurim, students, don't go Shabbos to the shuls, to chazer Chasidus. The Rebbe said he was very much astonished and surprised to see that nobody goes, so I should see to it that bochurim go.

CD   *At Yechidus did the Rebbe speak to you about Europe, the Holocaust, any of that?*

NM   No, nothing. The Rebbe asked me if I learned Tanach, Shulchan Aruch. In England I learned in Misnagdische, (non-Chasidic) Yeshivas. Tanach we didn't learn because it was more connected with Zionism. The Rebbe suggested that I learn Tanach, Shulchan Aruch, and also Hebrew grammar. I came back next time and the Rebbe asked me whether I learned every Shabbos Likutei Torah, the standard chasidic discourses on the weekly Torah portion. I told the Rebbe that I didn't learn it regularly. However, since I had to go to Shuls every week, I prepared my talks based on Likutei Torah. Remember, in those years there were no Likutei

Sichos [the Rebbe's explanations on the Torah portion, which were arranged from public addresses of previous years, edited in pamphlet form, and personally corrected and annotated by the Rebbe, which were distributed every week in the shuls and by mail] coming out so you made your own Droshos, sermons. So I went to the Likutei Torah of the Alter Rebbe on the weekly Torah portion.

CD   *You told the Rebbe that? What was the Rebbe's response?*

NM   Yes. My heart was beating, because in Yeshiva they taught us that a maamar should be Divrei Harav, words of the Rebbe, not your own thoughts. But I felt if I would say the maamor the way it is written, this would be difficult for the average Jew to understand. The ma'amorim in Likutei Torah have many difficult kabbalistic concepts. Therefore I decided to extract a nice question and answer and explain it well in my own words. So I told the Rebbe, I don't say the Likutei Torah maamor as it is written, but I take several points and from this I make a nice droshoh. I was afraid the Rebbe would admonish me. Instead, he said, "very good". He was very satisfied that I took several points from the discourse and made from it an entire sermon, even though I was not saying over verbatim the actual words of the Alter Rebbe.

CD   *At what point did you begin working on Chabad publications?*

NM   After my wedding. The Rebbe said I should prepare footnotes for the Alter Rebbe's Shulchan Aruch. He also instructed me to translate the second section of the Tanya, Shaar Hayichud vehaEmunah. I also edited the other parts of the Tanya. Some books are under my name and other books I didn't want under my name, so I wrote under pen names. Our People was not under my name, but the last four volumes I wrote.

CD   *Whose name is it under?*

122

NM   Jacob Issacs.

CD   *Why did you put the Tanya under your name and not that?*

NM   Anything I don't write myself from the beginning till the end, I don't put my name on. Tanya, the Siddur and the Machzor I translated from scratch, therefore my name is on them. Since the first volume of *Our People* was written by someone else, my name does not appear on any of the volumes.

CD   *The first thing you did were the footnotes on the Shulchan Aruch. How did you jump from doing a work which involved talmudic and chasidic scholarship to the English translations?*

NM   Yes, yes, yes, I was working all along on the footnotes to the Shulchan Aruch. Suddenly they called me up from the Hillel in New York. They wanted me to give a course in Jewish Mysticism, which would be a credited course in the college. So I asked the Rebbe, and he said yes, I should do it. They asked for a text. This was maybe 1969-70. There was no elaborate text on Chabad Chasidus in the English language. I needed to translate something. So I decided on the most philosophical part in Tanya, the *Shaar Hayichud vehaEmunah*. I translated each chapter and sent it to the Rebbe. He edited my translation. After the fifth, sixth or Seventh Chapter, the Rebbe said, "Now you know what I want."

CD   *Meaning?*

NM   The Rebbe was already satisfied. I had adopted his style. Now, he said, you can do the rest yourself. So I followed this style in translating the rest of *Shaar Hayichud vehaEmuna*. You asked me how I began translating works of chasidus? Simply, I was asked to give a course in college, and I needed a text.

CD   *So there was no translation of Tanya before that?*

NM   No.

CD   *Can you give one or two examples of the style the Rebbe taught you in translation and editing?*

NM   All right. The difficulty with Tanya is that you can have a sentence that goes on, and on, and it's hard to pick it up. There was one such very lengthy sentence, in the middle it said three times "vechulhu", (meaning "etc."). I left out one of the "etc.'s."

CD   *To make it flow?*

NM   Yes, instead of three, two. However, the Rebbe put it back in so it would be the precise translation of the original. Another example is the term "Doimem." The standard translation is "inanimate". In *Shaar Hayichud vehaEmuna* especially, he emphasizes there is no such thing as "inanimate." Everything has life. Since the standard translation is "inanimate", not just mineral but everything inanimate, so I translated "inanimate". The Rebbe wrote that the true translation is "silent" , it's not inanimate, only silent. So I translated "inanimate" and wrote in brackets "silent". The Rebbe took out the brackets around "silent" and put them around "inanimate". He was so precise. That was the Rebbe's style. Sometimes you have to sacrifice elegance of style for precision of meaning.

CD   *Do you think that was because it had to do with Tanya, the "Torah Shebiksav", the written Torah of Chasidus? In other words, if you were translating Likutei Torah, or a maamar, do you think the precision would be as necessary?*

NM   As far as the Rebbe's remark about "vechulhu", you can say it's a simple remark. For the "silent" comment there is a much deeper influence. The Rebbe wanted to emphasize that there is no such thing as dead things. Everything is alive, even a rock has a chayus, a life force, even though it can't move, it can't speak. There isn't such a thing as "inanimate." This is a misnomer. The Rebbe wanted to emphasize this teaching of Chasidus, that there isn't a thing without a "nitzutz Elokus" which is its soul, its Nefesh. How

124

can you translate something as inanimate? There is no such a thing.

CD   *I thought you were saying that the Rebbe wanted the precision of the translation.*

NM   That's one thing, but even more the meaning. Don't distort the meaning. There is no such a thing as inanimate. Everything has a soul. This is one of the fundamental teachings of chasidus. So if you don't translate properly you not only misconstrue and distort the meaning, but you are primarily transmitting something that is the opposite of what chasidus wants to teach. When you speak or you write you must be exact and not misinterpret. Everything has a soul. Remember, there's a Nefesh hatzomachas, a soul of the vegetative, a Nefesh hadoememus, a soul of the inanimate. Everything has a soul. Nothing is completely dead.

CD   *When you went into Yechidus those years, did you speak about issues of translation?*

NM   No. Many times the Rebbe started to speak to me about science which wasn't at all what I asked the Rebbe. For example, once the Rebbe spoke with me for over an hour and a half about evolution. The Rebbe discussed and explained at length the falsity of evolution, how, scientifically, not only from a Torah perspective, it is absurd. Over an hour and a half, almost two hours, without my mentioning anything on the subject. The Rebbe was saying how, eventually, I should deal with the outside world, with religious and scientific subjects. I never asked, I wouldn't ask the Rebbe such questions. On his own, he started to direct me in many such things. Eventually, when I had to deal with professors or go on television and so on, these would be vast challenges, so the Rebbe himself taught me these matters.

CD   *Mr. Potok wanted to know if the Rebbe had a private library in his house. Was there such a library and were the books marked up and annotated? His point was, he doesn't know if the Rebbe had an understanding of the way philology, philosophy, sociology works. You've had lengthy discussions with the Rebbe. I'd like to hear, in rational terms, about the Rebbe's knowledge of Philosophy, Science...*

NM   The Rebbe had enormous, enormous knowledge in every field. I'd like to give you an example. One of the students in the Yeshiva in Montreal, after he was ordained, decided to go to University, and he became a Ph.D. in Biochemistry. He had to write a dissertation, which you know has to be something original. He went to all the major biochemist's in the US, Stanford, Columbia, to find out what area would be good to investigate to contribute something original. After about a year of finding out which idea to pursue he chose a certain topic. He went to the Rebbe and said he is going to do research in this area. The Rebbe started to expound on this topic and told him everything what's known on this topic.

The Rebbe says, "in this research you will hit a dead end, like a wall, you won't be able to continue. You will have wasted so many years of research. Choose a different topic. " He came out and told me that this is absolutely and totally amazing. All of the professors, this is their chosen field. The Rebbe's chosen field is not chemistry or biochemistry. He had never seen anything like it. Professor Rosenbloom, of Columbia, a world-famous mathematician, how many times did he mention to me the Rebbe's incredible knowledge of mathematics?

Another example: A professor of English went in to the Rebbe. She teaches Shakespeare at Columbia University. She sat and discussed it with the Rebbe. The Rebbe quoted whole passages by heart! Sure, the Rebbe had a good memory but that this should be the Rebbe's interest, that is amazing. He quoted long passages by heart. I can understand the Rebbe memorizing Talmud and Chasidus. As Rabbi Hirschprung of Montreal testifies, when he went to the Rebbe for the first time he wasn't such a chasid. They were discussing Mishnayos, and the Rebbe quoted pages and pages of Tosefos Yom Tov by heart. However this woman told me the Rebbe quoted pages and pages of Shakespeare! You know about Shakespeare — such a difficult, difficult English.

CD   *What about philosophy? Plato, Aristotle.*

NM   You could see the Rebbe had all these philosophers in his pocket. Many times in his talks the Rebbe said "The Philosophers say this and this, but ...". The Rebbe knew not only Plato, Aristotle, Socrates, and the Pythagoreans, but also the Jewish Philosophers who were heretics, for example Philo of Alexandria. The Rebbe took them all into his pocket. The Rebbe's genius was in every area. He was not an architect, but his mind in mathematics, in logic, was so phenomenal. There was a person in Montreal who wanted to rebuild one of his buildings. He took the blueprints to the Rebbe, showing the garages, the offices, everything. The Rebbe looks through the blueprints. The Rebbe showed him why you don't go like this and like this, this would be much better. He comes back to Montreal and finds that by rearranging the building, the Rebbe had saved him $200,000!

     With his analytic mind, whatever the Rebbe undertook, immediately he was a Gaon in it, a genius. An example. You know it is explained in Chasidus, when you go up to the level of Yetzirah, you see Beriah much more clearly, just as when you go up in a balloon you see the stars more clearly. In the same vein the Rebbe, with his knowledge of Torah, he knew astronomy, physics. The Rebbe said nowadays, according to science, you can never prove the heliocentric or the geocentric hypothesis.

CD   *Is there a history to the translation of the Siddur?*

NM   Rabbi Hodakov requested that I translate it. The Rebbe must have gotten a lot of requests for a translation of the Chabad siddur.

CD   *You were working for Merkos?*

NM   All my life, only for Merkos. As a bochur, yet. I went in to Yechidus and I had a choice of several options, to go out in the world. The Rebbe looked through them and negated all of them. The Rebbe said he wanted to make a suggestion. I thought he meant a shiduch. The Rebbe said either to make the footnotes to the Shulchan Aruch, or in the Likutei Torah there are so many mistakes, and also footnotes are needed. I chose the Shulchan Aruch. The Rebbe said I should learn the whole Likutei Torah five times in one year. Each week I should learn five times the whole sedra in Likutei Torah. I should know it clear. This is an average of thirty pages. The Rebbe said this is all in addition to my regular scheduled Torah classes. All of this should be learned after Yeshiva hours. I said to the Rebbe, "Likutei Torah I know... Shulchan Aruch I don't know..."

The Rebbe asked me three times to work for him; as a student, before my wedding, and then when I went for my Ph.D. One of those three times, the Rebbe said something incredible — that if only we would finish half of the work before Moshiach comes. The Rebbe said, "we" including my work as part of his work. The Rebbe's modesty — he could make everybody feel needed.

CD   *Did you have annotations from the Rebbe on the Siddur?*

NM   No, because after the Tanya the Rebbe said I was on my own. But I sent to the Rebbe samples of translated pages on the siddur. The Rebbe annotated on the very first page, "Koton me shehigiya ledaber yomar...", with three dots. That's what it said in Loshon Hakodesh. So I translated it, "A minor who begins speaking says as follows" instead of just "says..." The Rebbe writes in his remark, "when a child starts to speak, can he already say the whole page?" This page was added to the Tehillas Hashem (Chabad) siddur by the Rebbe. In the original Tehillas Hashem Siddur it wasn't there. This is the Rebbes translation. The first time the siddur came out in the United States the Rebbe added the entire page. So the Rebbe knew what he meant. So the Rebbe edited this page of my translation on the siddur. I wrote a introduction to the English version of the siddur and sent into the Rebbe.

CD   *Yes, I read the introduction. It is very nice. He gave it a checkmark?*

NM   That's it! I sent in the example pages, and the Rebbe made slight, slight emendations.

CD   *The translation of G-d's name. Did the Rebbe have anything to do with that?*

NM   No, but on that very page where the Rebbe made corrections he didn't make any corrections on my translation of Hashem's name from the Hebrew into English. When some people questioned the exact translation of Hashem's name, I went to Reb Zalman Shimon, the Rav of the Lubavitcher community. I told him, "Please give me a ruling. Is this correct or not?" I explained the whole thing. He said I was right.

Even though the Rav made his ruling, those people felt since the Rav didn't know the English language that well therefore they called Rabbi Zalman Posner, who knows English and is also a Rav and a translator of many books. So he dials, and Zalman says, yes, it's correct. Then I went to Rabbi Hodakov, and I showed him that this is the responsum of Rabbi Zalman Shimon. So Rabbi Hodakov goes to the Rebbe.

The whole time the Rebbe had on his desk the whole page, on which he had made corrections and didn't change the translation of the name of Hashem. The Rebbe answered, "Tell Nissan Mangel he shouldn't be bothered by all the objections. Let him go back to his work. " The Rebbe disregarded it completely.

CD   *I know you translated the Rosh Hashana and Yom Kippur machzorim, prayer books. Could you tell me how this come about?*

NM   The translation of the Machzor was something very interesting. I was invited to speak in Oxford, England. Just before I left, it was the chasidic holiday of 12 Tammuz. Rabbi Yudel Krinsky calls me up and says he has something very important to show me from the Rebbe. The Rebbe had given him a note, for me. I remember I told Krinsky that I would rather wait to see the note upon my return from England. I felt if I had seen the note before I left on my trip, I would never get to England because the Rebbe probably wanted something translated now and I had committed myself already to the lecture in Oxford.

I asked Krinsky, without knowing what the note said, if I could do it right now, before I went to Oxford for a week. He said, "when you come back, then do it." I came back and the Rebbe's note said that I should translate the Chabad Machzor and it should be finished by Rosh Hashanah so that people can use this English version for Rosh Hashana and Yom Kippur. Believe me, for me it was as impossible as if you should tell me, "climb up the wall to the ceiling." And the way I translate, I don't translate just hop-hop-hop. It has to be precise, people are davenning in English, it has to be a kosher Siddur.

It was impossible because you have to translate, edit, I don't have a staff. I did everything myself. Afterwards it has to be printed, bound, how much time do I have? I wrote to the Rebbe that it is impossible for me to have it fully translated by Rosh Hashanah. The Rebbe replies, "There is no such thing as impossible. Yogaita umatzasa (if you try you will succeed)." Those were the Rebbe's words. So I worked day and night. Usually I would translate, my wife would type it, I would edit it again, and then I would give it to the printer. Here I had no time to type it up. And it came back, I had to polish it up on the spot. At the beginning of Elul it was already printed, and by Chai Elul it was already bound. Boruch Hashem there was such a Siyata diShmaya, help from Hashem. When it came out, it was sent all over the world, like Australia, South Africa, etc. I got a telegram about only one printing mistake, "nisuch hayayin" is "wine libation"; instead it read "swine libation"!

This was the only mistake! It wasn't my mistake, it was a printing mistake. It was a Siyata diShmaya all through. When the Rebbe says you can do it, believe me, even if it's to jump up on the roof, you can do it! Someone once said to the Rebbe, "Rebbe what you ask of me is impossible. If you asked me to jump down form the roof, I could do it—if you ask me to go up again, how could I do it?" The Rebbe says, "You could climb up also." I am a witness to this. The Machzor for Yom Kippur! The piyutim, with the Avodah. I wanted to write an introduction, what is teshuvah, what are the Yomim Noraim, however there was no time.

CD *So how do you reconcile the Rebbe's view of the Conservative movement and at the same time his support of such people as Dimetrofsky and Mandelbaum being at the Seminary?*

NM   The Rebbe utilized every person. The Rebbe tried to get them to pull the Conservative movement to the right. As you know, if a person does one mitzvah, and you can accomplish that this person should do two mitzvos, wonderful. He never sanctioned or endorsed. The Rebbe encouraged every person's talents.

CD *Were you involved with people at Jewish Theological Seminary?*

NM   I was involved as a student in Montreal. Students who had to be ordained from Jewish Theological Seminary used to come to Montreal, and they would learn twelve pages of Gemorah Brochos with Rashi. So I met a number of them. Afterwards, the Rebbe sent me there, several times, to share with them words of Torah.

CD *You knew Rabbi Lieberman?*

NM   I met him. I didn't have anything to do with him.

CD *Was he known as a genius?*

NM   He was a Gaon, at least in Bekius, fluent in the talmud.

CD *In the Jerusalem talmud as well?*

NM   He knew Yerushalmi. He was a Gaon. His dissertation was a biur on Pesikhta d'Rav Kahana. Everything is Divine Providence. Even though he made changes to the traditional approach to halacha, yet he also pulled the conservative movement and the seminary to the right. In his private life he was orthodox, a very hard position to be in.

CD *The issue about the Rebbe and Moshiach — can you explain it in a logical intelligent way? The Jewish world did not have a big problem with believing or allowing us to believe that the Rebbe could be Moshiach during his lifetime. I say that because I've discussed it with non-Lubavitcher people and they acknowledged it. But now that the Rebbe's passed on physically, the whole notion is so unconventional, even if you find support statements in the Zohar or Gemorah, it's just so unconventional, that people are not able to handle such an esoteric idea. Do you see this as a good, healthy thing for the Jewish people?*

NM The question should be put differently. Is it a true thing or not? If it's Emes, there is nothing wrong with saying it. If it's not Emes, you shouldn't do it. The question is, is it authentic or not authentic?

It is not my philosophy that we have to go out and get everyone to believe and feel the way I do. Many times, when the Rebbe was with us in a physical sense, people asked me "What is your belief in the Rebbe's being Moshiach?" My response was always to say, "I'm not here to sell who is Moshiach. If you are comfortable with somebody else, it is perfectly well with me. If you want to believe this Tzaddik, or Rebbe, or Gaon, is Moshiach, that's fine." The only thing that I try to communicate is that we should believe in Moshiach and in the coming of Moshiach, as the Rebbe said in the name of the Midrash, "the time of your redemption has come." You don't have to wait 2000 years, 200 years, 20 years, Moshiach is on the way. That's all that I try to sell.

But I can very easily defend those people who say the Rebbe is Moshiach and can also explain it halachically, logically, even though some people have difficulty accepting it. Anything which is novel, a person has a natural aversion and difficulty accepting it. A simple, physical example: If you are in a cold swimming pool, and go into a lukewarm pool, you will feel very warm. Everything is relative to where you were before. The same from a hot mikva to a lukewarm one. You would feel very cold. If you had said to your Bobbe and Zaide, you can cross the ocean in a plane,

then they elaborate. The Torah says Yesh m'Ayin, creation ex nihi-
lo, so we ask ourselves why Yesh m'Ayin, why not ilah v'olul,
cause and effect. So you have the deepest ideas in philosophy, but
they are rooted and anchored in truth. Aristotle wasn't rooted in
truth. And today many of those ideas are being disproved. You can
only draw a perfectly round circle if you stick a compass into a
solid thing which doesn't allow it to drift. However, if you draw the
circle free hand, it will go off on tangents. You are not rooted in
anything concretely.

We start out with a Torah. Torah says the world is Yesh
m'Ayin, not evolution. Then I try to use my intellect to prove that.
The counterarguments are logical, but I use my mind to prove this
Emes. Here, Chaim, you trust me. Because Torah starts with a kernel of truth, I know this is the emes. Here too, the Rebbe's ideas are
emes. If there are questions, I look in the midrash, the Zohar,
Kabbalah, Chasidus, a Sicha. Why do I search — because I know I
have the nekudas haemes, the truth.

CD   *Are you saying that an intelligent person would agree with
what your saying?*

NM   Most people never learned the last two chapters of
Rambam, where he elaborates on the details of Moshiach, the who,
what, when, and where. I remember once the Rebbe said that even
some Roshei Yeshivos never learned the last chapters of Rambam.
So many of the ideas that Moshiach is some kind of Malach, Angel,
comes from a persons childhood. No one ever had a problem
believing that when Moshiach comes he will come from heaven!
Everyone always believed Eliyahu would come to usher in
Moshiach. Where does Eliyahu come from? From heaven! And
does anyone have any problem with that?! This is the hypocrisy.
It's intuitively accepted. So Eliyahu can come from heaven but
Moshiach can't!

A prophet like Eliyahu, will come from heaven. This
Halacha says. A prophet is a human being of flesh and blood.
Therefore why can't the Rebbe, who has the status of a prophet,
come back as Moshiach?

CD   *Let me ask you, isn't it implied in many places that Moshiach is someone who is alive?*

NM   Only the Rambam.

CD   *But isn't the Rambam the final Halachic authority on issues dealing with Moshiach?*

NM   Yes, however there are many additional insights mentioned in the kabbalah that are necessary to know. It says in the writings of the Arizal, based on the Zohar, that Moshe Rabbeinu is goel rishon, the first redeemer. Hashem gave him a mission, he didn't die, his soul went up to heaven. In the same vein the beginning is not that someone is Moshiach, he is only fit to be Moshiach. Afterwards he gets the Neshomah of Moshiach, and some people know and accept that he is Moshiach. Then he passes away. Then he comes back and the whole world knows that he is Moshiach. For instance, when there was a Sanhedrin, Rabbi Yehoshua ben Levi was asked who is Moshiach? The Baal Shem Tov spoke to the Neshomah of Moshiach. When Eliyahu HaNavi told Rabbi Yehoshua ben Levi that Moshiach was sitting at the gate of Rome, how do these statements accord with the fact that Moshiach has to be of flesh and blood? The Arizal explains based on the Zohar, that Moshiach is a general soul, Yechidah. The Neshomah comes down, and then he, and a few people, know that he is Moshiach. And afterwards he will go away.

CD   *You still haven't gotten to Techiyas Hamesim!*

NM   Wait! He doesn't have to have Techiyas Hamesim! Moshe left his body in Yetzirah or Beriyah and his neshomah went up to Atzilus. Not Techiyas Hamesim!

CD   *But Moshe was in his physical body.*

NM   No! It says explicitly not. Moshe Rabbeinu went up with his body to Yetzirah during the giving of the Torah. Begashmiyus, physically he disappeared. The body has to go to Yetzirah, Beriyah, to get the neshomah of Moshiach.

CD   *Okay. So based on that, why can't the Satmar Rebbe or the Previous Lubavitch Rebbe come as Moshiach?*

NM   I have no problem with that. I am not here to say who is Moshiach. If you ask me why I believe it's the Rebbe, I can answer you. It's simple. Whatever I say in Chasidic philosophy has to be based on Torah. All my beliefs are connected with Torah. Why did Moshe get the Torah? The midrash says that the Aibershter told him that even though Avrohom Avinu is much greater than you, you are going to get the Torah because you are the seventh generation, and all sevens are beloved. Because it's the same idea as Shabbos — being a mekabel — Shabbos receives from the whole week but nevertheless it's greater.

The Rebbe said this is the seventh generation. So we know that it's counted from the Alter Rebbe. What if we start from the Baal Shem Tov and say that the Rebbe Rashab is the Moshiach? The Previous Lubavitch Rebbe said of his father that he is the Kos Shel Brocha of all the Rebbeim, he is the seventh generation from the Baal Shem Tov. So he could be the Moshiach! Why is it we maintain it is the Rebbe? Because, the Rebbe says in his first maamor that we are the seventh generation. How is that possible if we begin counting from the Baal Shem Tov? The explanation is that we don't start with the Baal Shem Tov but rather with the Alter Rebbe. Subsequently the Rebbe is the seventh. This hints that he is the Moshiach of the generation.

The function of Moshiach is, the world will be full of the knowledge of G-d, all flesh will see and perceive G-d. Can you start with the Baal Shem Tov, when the revelation of G-d has to be not just general, but inward, as was accomplished with the Alter Rebbe and Chasidus Chabad? That's what the Rebbe says, that general Chasidus is "makifim", short aphorisms, inspirations. To bring it into "wisdom, understanding, and knowledge", that's Chabad. When you explain it there are no questions and no fanaticism.

CD   *How did you believe in Moshiach as a holocaust survivor?*

NM   Because I listen to the Rebbe's of Lubavitch and learn chasidus. An ordinary Jew has always believed in Moshiach, Ani Maamin. Without Chasidus, it's peripheral, not affecting and guiding ones perception and action on a regular basis. Chasidus makes it real.

10

Rabbi Menachem Porush
Former Knesset member representing the Agudas Israel Party

BRIDGING THE GAP IN JERUSALEM

CD   *Can you please give me a brief history of yourself, your position in the Knesset, and your first encounter with the Rebbes of Lubavitch?*

MP   My father visited Rabbi Yosef Yitzchok, the sixth Lubavitcher Rebbe in Riga shortly after the Rebbe had been freed from his arrest in 1928. The Rebbe said that he was very much encouraged by a visit from a Jew from Jerusalem.

My first personal contact was on a special mission for the Brisker Rov. When he heard I was going to America in 1948, he asked me to request the influence of the Rebbe on Zalman Shazar, at that time the minister of education. Shazar still went by the name of Rubashov. There were people who wanted to change the language and the curriculum of the Yiddish-speaking religious schools. The Brisker Rov was completely opposed to this.

When I came in to the Rebbe, he said right away, "Porush has several perushim [meanings]. One of them belongs to Neturei Karta, one belongs to Mizrachi, and one belongs to Agudas Yisroel. To whom do you belong?"

It is true that I have relatives in all these parties. I told him that I am the son of Moshe Porush of the Agudah. He said immediately, "Oh this is the man who greeted me right after I was freed from the arrest. It was one of the first visits after I was freed, and it was especially important for me, coming from a Yerushalmi from generations back."

I told him that I have a mission from the Brisker Rov to the Rebbe. He repeated several times, "The Brisker Rov sends a mission to me!?" He asked me to explain the situation. I told him that with the establishment of the state, the government wanted to control all schools. They didn't want the Talmud Torah's learning in Yiddish to be different from all the other schools. The danger was great. He agreed: Without government approval these schools would lose their financial support.

The Rebbe told me, "Go see Shazar and tell him that I want him to fulfill the request of the Brisker Rov, and I am sure the Rubashov family in Israel will not shame the Rubashov family in Russia. This will be enough for him to understand that he has to fulfill what I want." The morning after I returned to Eretz Yisroel, I went right to the Knesset to see Shazar. I told him what the Rebbe had said. He started to jump from one member of the Knesset to another, telling them that he has special regards from the Lubavitcher Rebbe. This helped. This was a great, great influence on Shazar for maintaining the Yiddish-speaking schools.

This was a very great help. The Brisker Rov was very satisfied.

CD   *Zalman Shazar was born a Lubavitcher. He was connected to the previous Rebbe as a young boy in Russia, and in his later years he became really close to the Rebbe. I understand he became observant. What was going on in the middle years?*

MP   He he had a split personality. Late Shabbos afternoon, he used to drive his car close to Shaarey Chesed, park there, and then walk to the synagogue for "Sholosh Seudos", the late meal on Shabbos afternoon. Rabbi Charlap used to say Torah, and sing with great enthusiasm. Shazar would really get into the Zemiros and Nigunim. He would sing along with great fervor and enthusiasm, but he still came in a car.

He was not only an interesting person, you could see the struggle in his soul was like Jacob and Esau. When he spoke about Lubavitch, he became another person.

RD   *What was your first contact with the present Rebbe?*

MP   At that time I used to visit America twice a year. I was in Philadelphia for Shabbos, and we heard on the radio that the Lubavitcher Rebbe had passed away. The train to New York was full of people from all over America going to the funeral. I was very much moved.

When this Rebbe was appointed, I got a very close connection right away. I used to visit him twice a year, right before I would go back to Israel. Before Rosh Hashanah, and before Pesach. Sitting together the day before Rosh Hashanah, he would remember everything we had discussed before Pesach, and everything that had happened in Eretz Yisroel in the six months. He was inside the picture. I used to be with him one and a half hours, one time two hours and 45 minutes.

CD   *What was it like in the early years, the 1950's?*

MP   At that time, there was friction between Agudas Yisroel and Lubavitch regarding education. Lubavitch continued with the system of education under the supervision of the mamlachat dati. At that time was established Chinuch Atzmai, which had the support of the Agudah. In many places there were clashes between the two systems.

It was a very tense situation between Lubavitch and the ruling council of the Agudah. My interest was to bridge this gap. Once the Lubavitcher Rebbe told me, "You're going back to Eretz Yisroel. Ask Yechezkel Sarna if he wants to bring up again the controversy between the Vilna Gaon and the Baal Shem Tov." Yechezkel Sarna answered me, "He can be the Baal Shem Tov. I don't feel that I can be the Gaon."

Although you know Reb Aron Kotler's attitude, he knew about my visits with the Lubavitcher Rebbe, and expressed his happiness that there was someone who could bring understanding between the Agudah's position and the Lubavitcher Rebbe's view.

CD   *At one time the Rebbe was interested in combining all of the religious parties into one bloc. Did you discuss this with the Rebbe?*

MP   He insisted that Agudas Yisroel should vote with the Mizrachi.

The Brisker Rov was very strongly against this. He told me once, even if there were a danger of Yeshiva students serving in the army, or of girls serving in the army, uniting with Mizrachi would be the greatest danger!

"So far?" I asked him. He said that if the Mizrachi were to get 60% of a united religious party, then the advisory council of the Agudah, the Moetzes Gedolei Hatorah, would in actuality have no say at all. He saw this as the greatest danger to Yiddishkeit.

The Lubavitcher Rebbe was interested in a religious bloc. It would provide more votes and more influence, but the Gedolei Yisroel's attitude was very much influenced by the Brisker Rov. The Rebbe many times told me, "I know you, I know your influence. You can arrange that it should be as I want it."

CD   *Could you?*

MP   The attitude of Reb Aron Kotler was originally like the attitude of the Lubavitcher Rebbe. When I brought the message of the Brisker Rov, which was against uniting with Mizrachi, I came to Fleishman in the mountains, where Reb Aron Kotler stayed for the summer. I told him the message. He paced back and forth 6 or 8 times on the porch, his face was on fire. He said, "Nu, he has given his ruling and I cannot go against it." So Reb Aron was also against the coalition.

To tell you the truth, the Rebbe was very upset that I didn't go around the Brisker Rov and Reb Aron Kotler. But I felt I couldn't. He thought my power was greater but I knew that was the situation.

CD   *Apparently the Rebbe felt that if you had tried a little harder you would have gotten extra help from upstairs. What was your own opinion on the subject?*

MP   At that time, I couldn't understand why the Lubavitcher Rebbe wanted this. Then, Mizrachi was much worse. Of the two flags, nationalism and religion, the flag of religion was down, not like the nationalism. It was difficult to work with them in the Knesset. But that was the most difficult time in my public life, between the influence of the Lubavitcher Rebbe and the Gedolei Yisroel, and the National Religious Party. Later on, the Lubavitcher Rebbe didn't have this enthusiastic interest for the unity of Mizrachi and Agudas Yisroel.

CD   *They didn't unite in the end. Do you think the the result was good?*

MP   In my opinion, 35 years later, going together is nice, but it's more practical to go separately. It's difficult during election time, but later on we have much more votes, through not going together.

CD   *It seems to me that you're a moderate, a middle-of- the-roader. Is that a correct summary of your political outlook?*

MP   Yes, yes, that's it. As the Mishne says, "Don't judge a person till you come to his place." I am always taking into account how each person was raised, under which influences, who was his teacher and mentor. Otherwise I wouldn't be able to have achieved what I have achieved. Thank G-d, I have achieved a lot.

CD   *The Rebbe took a strong stand in the 1990 election. What was your involvement in this?*

MP   We are very grateful for his help of when we split with Degel in 1990. At that time we felt tremendous gratitude to the Lubavitcher Rebbe for the great help he gave to Agudas Yisroel in the elections, bringing great success.
    Later on, we were not satisfied with the Likud, not happy at all. We were very happy when Begin was Prime Minister, very unhappy when Shamir took over. We came to a decision that we

have to go over to the socialist bloc. But, since the Lubavitcher Rebbe gave us such great help, it was unthinkable to do it without consulting him. It was already very difficult to get an appointment, but I went to America and spoke with him. He told me to follow the advice of the Gedolei Yisroel in Eretz Yisroel, to put in writing the reasons for their decisions. He said he would answer in writing. I have the answers.

Whenever I wrote strongly against the Likud, he wrote, "and you expect that Labor will not disappoint you?" I have this in writing, on a copy of my note to him.

Therefore, I went to the Maarach. There were two meetings of Moetzes Gedolei HaTorah, one five hours, and the other six, and they decided to go with the socialist bloc. I told them what the Rebbe had said. I told them that if he had told us positively we shouldn't do it, we shouldn't do it. Remember, we owed him tremendous gratitude for what he did for us.

CD   *Did you eventually reconcile things with Shamir?*

MP   When we made the resolution for Begin we were very satisfied, just as we are now very happy with Ehud Olmert. The change was when Begin left and Shamir came in. He was very not nice. That brought us to go over and negotiate with the socialists. But these negotiations did not work, because we lost the Mizrachi party with Werdiger. Then, we started negotiations with Likud and Shamir, and this time there was an entire change, a real change. He was ready to help, interested.

He saw that we can make a revolution. Shamir is a very interesting man, not a simple person. He's a man of the machteret, the underground. He's not charming, he is not a personality, but he knows how to handle matters secretly.

CD   *All the time. What is your opinion on how to deal with the so-called "peace process" going on now? They want to give away so much of the country.*

MP   Things are bad. I've followed what goes on in Israel since the Balfour declaration. I can't recall a time I felt worse than today. Very bad. Agudas Yisroel doesn't have too much to sell. We have only one representative in the Knesset. The other three...

CD *I understand that you have also had experience with the Rebbes of Belz and Satmar.*

MP When we went to America for Chinuch Atzmai, Reb Aron of Belz was still alive. On a Saturday night I went to his "Tisch". He was still sitting at Sholosh Seudos. His assistant told him I was traveling to America and wanted his blessing. He gave me his blessing, "You *will* be successful, you *should* be successful, and you *must* be successful."

This was a triple blessing, three expressions of success. He then proceeded to give me three small challohs from his plate.

I came to America. Reb Aron Kotler said to me, "You're coming to America in the summer? In the summer nothing gets accomplished. Go to Mexico." I went there for a week, but I made no money. I needed to raise money to pay the Chinuch Atzmai teachers. Right before Shabbos, I bought a lottery ticket. I was sure I would win the lottery, so I was able to start Shabbos happily, like you're supposed to. Immediately after Shabbos, I ran out to see if I won or not. I had not, I was very disappointed. I went to see Reb Moshe Rothfeld. He said to leave him alone, he had things to do. I said the whole book of Psalms, I was really crying. The next day I started collecting. I made $85,000 that week.

I met a Jew in Mexico who asked me, "There is a Jew in Israel called Aron Rokeach, did he pass away?" I understood he meant the Belzer Rebbe, who had just given me his blessing. I was in a state of shock.

Since I was in Mexico, I could not go to the funeral. In America I heard Rabbi Yonasan Steiff give the eulogy at the memorial service. A strong eulogy, with tears. There was a feeling as though we had personally been present at his passing away.

When I told the Satmar Rebbe that the Belzer Rebbe passed on, he was in pain. He said, " The Belzer Rebbe, who supported and encouraged voting in the Israeli elections, was no longer around to retract his position. So for eternity his words would remain this way. How terrible!"

Regardless of his views, he gave me of his time. He even gave us a check for Chinuch Atzmai.

CD *Your family has been in this country for seven generations, and you already have great-grandchildren, which makes ten generations. You have met so many giants of Torah. How did the Lubavitcher Rebbe stand out to you?*

MP With respect to intuition, there is no comparison to him. With the feeling of responsibility for all Jews and every Jew, every individual, no comparison. For him an individual matter had meaning like an entire world. Once he told me, "See Menachem, you yourself have a connection to Lubavitch, does your family have some connection to Lubavitch?" I told him that my father remarried a woman who was a Chaimson, a Lubavitcher family. Whenever I came back from America, she was in heaven — because I had been by the Lubavitcher Rebbe.

The Rebbe said, "on your return, I would like you right away to ask your father if your family has some connection to Lubavitch. You will find out. Don't put it off, because you will forget. Ask him right after you greet him." Then the Rebbe gave me a little Tanya.

As soon as I saw my father, I told him what the Lubavitcher Rebbe had asked. He told me that the father of my grandmother used to memorize and repeat the Chasidic discourses of the third Lubavitcher Rebbe, the "Tzemach Tzedek". This was an official position. His family name was Itkin.

That which was, is no longer.

I had the great privilege to know the Chazon Ish, the Tcherbiner Rov, the Brisker Rov, the Mirrer Rosh Yeshiva, the Beis Yisroel, the former Belzer Rebbe. However the Lubavitcher Rebbe was totally unique.

His specialty, besides his power of intuition, was his love for each Jew. Once I was sitting with him 5 hours at a Farbrengen on Shabbos Hagodol. I was much surprised by his intuition and his feeling responsibility for each of Klal Yisroel, each individual. When it comes to holiness, I'm no judge of who is and who is not a holy person, but I'll tell you this: When we spoke about complicated practical matters, which by most people, the biggest minds in Torah included, took a lot of explaining, he understood them right away. I didn't have to finish my sentences. He knew everyone, religious people, secular people, all of the leaders.

CD   *Yesterday you told me that the Rebbe once told you that your love for Eretz Yisroel...*

MP   ...is so strong that all of the scandalous iniquities do not affect it. This is right. I can tell you that I was in a state of absolute religious terror before going in to see the Rebbe. After being in with him you cannot imagine my state. It took me days and weeks to digest it.

When I spoke with the Lubavitcher Rebbe I was astonished about how he knows everything, especially about what was going on in Eretz Yisroel. although I didn't get all of what he was saying right away. When I would walk out, I would start thinking, "what did he mean with this?" As time went on I began to realize that he was right, that this is the way we have to do things. I used to stay in very close contact. Telephone, letters, I would say he gave me great confidence.

11

Mr. Chaim Potok
Author of *The Chosen* and *My Name Is Asher Lev*

ARTISTIC DETACHMENT AND JUDAISM

CD *How did you first meet with the Rebbe? Was it in private or at a farbrengen?*

CP As I told you, I never met the Rebbe in private. I met the Rebbe twice at Farbrengen's and once at a Mincha service. It must have been in the 70's. All 3 times, if I remember correctly, I was accompanied by Rabbi Shemtov. The second Farbrengen I sat up in front with a large group of others, and spoke to the Rebbe in front of all the people there. I was at the time the editor of the Jewish Publication Society. His words to me were, "Remember to put the Jewish back in the Jewish Publication Society." We always published books that had to with Jewish scholarship, Jewish history, Jewish thought. Therefore, I wasn't entirely sure what he meant. That was the second time I met him. We stayed, my wife and I, very late that night, and we also heard the Rebbe speaking Chasidus. It was about 2-3 o'clock in the morning.

Then I met the Rebbe at a Mincha service, when a group of Yeshiva boys were about to leave on a worldwide mission. He noticed me and nodded. After the Mincha service the students gathered around him. He gave them a Brocha and he went away.

CD *You didn't talk to him on that occasion?*

CP No.

CD   *Did you understand what he meant about, "Remember to put the 'Jewish' back in the Jewish Publication Society"? Did you ask him?*

CP   There was no opportunity to ask him, because there were others waiting to speak to him. It was very puzzling to me.

CD   *The first time you came, Rabbi Shemtov introduced you to the Rebbe?*

CP   If I remember correctly, he knew that I was coming. I had just written either The Promise or *My Name Is Asher Lev*. He knew that I was a novelist, but said nothing to me about the novels. The conversation lasted longer than with all the others who came before me, and some staff people seemed to be annoyed that I was taking so much of the Rebbe's time. One or two of them came over to me and asked, "What did the Rebbe say?", so I told them what I'm telling you now.

CD   *What motivated you to go see the Rebbe?*

CP   First, I grew up in a world of Chasidus and Chasidism. My mother was a direct descendant of one of the sons of the Rizhiner. Her father was a Chortkover and my father was a Belzer. My uncle was a Belzer. The whole family comes from that world. Second, I became especially interested in Lubavitch because my wife grew up at 576 Eastern Parkway. She had seen Lubavitch expand in that neighborhood, had seen that neighborhood transformed from a middle class neighborhood to a Chasidic neighborhood. I was very curious about that. And, my in-laws still lived at 576 Eastern Parkway, so when I visited them, I would see Lubavitch every-where. After I wrote The Chosen and The Promise — I had always been interested in art - I began to think about the possibility of writ-ing a story about an artist who had grown up in a very religious world. It was at that point that Rabbi Shemtov walked into my office one day.

My interest in that subject and Rabbi Shemtov came together, and the focus became Lubavitch, although I wasn't particularly interested in writing specifically about Lubavitch. What a writer does is research and become very familiar with a specific world and subject. Then the imagination takes over. So the streets where my wife grew up, became the focus of my interest, and since Lubavitch was still on those streets, it all came together into the *Asher Lev* story. When Rabbi Shemtov invited me to come to a Farbrengen, I said sure, let me see what's going on, and we went.

CD   *Had you studied the philosophy and history of Lubavitch before that?*

CP   Yes, I knew a great deal about its philosophy and its leaders. I had studied that mostly on my own during and after my student years at the Jewish Theological Seminary.

CD   *So you are a graduate of Jewish Theological Seminary?*

CP   Of Yeshiva University, and the Seminary.

CD   *So you knew Rabbi Lieberman.*

CP   He was my teacher.

CD   *So you met the Rebbe. What impression do you retain?*

CP   I had the impression that he was a very charismatic leader, a man who could use his knowledge and his personality to build and to lead a movement of Chasidism. I could see the control he had over the group, I could see the awe, respect, and reverence that all the people there had for him.

CD   *You never corresponded with him?*

CP   No.

CD   *I'm sure you've met many other Jewish leaders throughout your life. How did the Rebbe compare? What is his niche, in your opinion?*

CP   There is no one comparable to the Rebbe in Yeshiva life, because it isn't the nature of a Yeshiva Rov to build an empire, as it were. A Yeshiva Rov will try to get his talmidim to teach in other Yeshivos; he will not try to build a vast, international empire of followers. The great Yeshiva Rabbonim in Europe built mostly around Yeshivos.

Lubavitch, however, had a charismatic leader, chosen by a previous leader, who apparently sensed something in this leader and chose him for the specific purpose of rebuilding a world, shattered by the Second World War. Somehow that sense of possibility has proven to be true; the Rebbe succeeded and built an empire, a worldwide movement.

The Jewish leaders that I know are politicians in Israel, United States , senators, congressmen, judges, and great Rabbonim. There is a difference between the Rebbe and those leaders: the Rebbe created a worldwide movement with dedicated, devoted, followers, who not only listened attentively but waited eagerly for anything that he had to say. There were in the 30's in the United States a number of charismatic leaders, religious and political, like Abba Hillel Silver and Stephen Wise, but that period pretty much ended after the Second World War.

CD   *You see the worldwide movement of Lubavitch as a direct result of the Rebbe's charisma?*

CP   Well, if you say that before the Rebbe there was no worldwide Lubavitch movement, and after the Rebbe there is a worldwide Lubavitch movement, then obviously the Rebbe had something to do with it. Whether you agree with this or that position of the Rebbe or this or that position of the movement, the fact remains that the movement exists now when it didn't exist before his presence.

CD *Have you witnessed Lubavitch in other parts of the country and the world?*

CP I have come across Lubavitch in many cities of the United States, Canada, Paris, Nice, Singapore, Hong Kong, Rome, Australia. It is certainly a presence that has to be reckoned with in Judaism, and it didn't exist when I was growing up. So, one has to say that the Rebbe generated this worldwide movement.

CD *So, in your opinion, the Gerer Rebbe in the 30's with, some say, hundreds of thousands of Chasidim, would you call him a charismatic leader?*

CP They are all charismatic leaders — the question is what the leader does with his charisma, what his aim is. There are more Satmarer Chasidim than there are Lubavitch Chasidim, but nobody says that the Satmarer Chasidim are a force in Jewish life. For very specific historical reasons, the Lubavitch movement in Russia in the last century turned in the direction of "evangelizing", missionizing the Jewish people. That missionizing tendency remained in Lubavitch when it moved to the United States. The Rebbe began to rebuild Lubavitch, and he used that as the essential instrumentality for goal-directing the movement. And he used it with singular success.

CD *What historical reasons?*

CP To avoid the conscription policy of Czar Nicholas I. Because if you went to Yeshiva, you weren't conscripted. Those policies were terrible as far as Jews were concerned, because you ended up in the army of Russia for 25 years of your life and very often you were conscripted at a very early age. The essential goal of that Conscription policy, from 1825 to 1855, was to Christianize Jewish children. We know precisely what the Rebbe of those times did. His goal was to get his Chasidim to create yeshivos, get children into those yeshivos, and thereby avoid having them serve in the army of the Czar.

That's the turning point in Lubavitch, because it wasn't a missionizing movement before that point. It was another Chasidic movement, an intellectual Chasidic movement, but it didn't have this powerful, thrusting goal at its core, that is to say the "conversion of the Jews." The later Rebbes realized how successful you could be with this ethic, and that you could get a community to work toward this ethic, to unite behind this ethic. Rabbi Schneerson was especially creative in this regard.

CD   *Does it seem that all branches of Judaism are incorporating more of that approach?*

CP   Yes, I think that outreach, as we now call it, has become a major thrust in Jewish life today. To the extent that all the groups in Judaism succeed, I think to that extent Lubavitch is owed a measure of gratitude — one recognizes that it was among the very first that went out to bring Jews in. I make no bones about the fact that Lubavitch's main purpose is to convert the whole Jewish people, if it can, to Lubavitch.

CD   *You believe that?*

CP   Oh yes. Since it cannot do that, it will settle for second, third, and fourth best, wherever it can. Also, perhaps, psychologically it doesn't want to do that, because if everybody becomes Lubavitch then Lubavitch disappears. One of the strengths of any Chasidic movement is its separateness.

CD   *Uniqueness.*

CP   So you have that ambivalent goal. But every group has that ambivalent goal. It wants the world to accept its ideas and at the same time wants to remain unique. I don't fault Lubavitch for wanting every Jew to become a fundamentalist Jew. At the same time, it has saved lives, it has taken kids out of the streets. It doesn't always do things neatly and cleanly but then who does.

CD   *Do you believe Lubavitch can create Chaim Potoks?*

CP   No.

CD   *Why not?*

CP   I think it does not want to. It cannot create Chaim Potoks who stay inside the group, because in order to write with total objectivity, or with as much objectivity as one can muster, you have to look at whatever you are, from the outside. The part of a Chaim Potok it can create is the cortex, the core. Without that a human being is nothing. But there are other parts to a human being, and that's all the things that come to a human being after the original core is formed. It's a very big world that we live in, a very rich and troubling culture, and if you want to be an artist, you have to learn as much about that world as you possibly can, and communicate with it. Lubavitch can create the core of a Chaim Potok or an Asher Lev, but Chaim Potok and Asher Lev will ultimately have to leave it.

CD   *Asher Lev is the Chasid who rebels?*

CP   And is constantly inside and outside his community, constantly part of and not part of it, constantly be confronting people in the group who will wish that he would leave. It is endless ambivalence.

CD   *You're saying that in order to really appreciate, understand, something one must be outside for a while, for objectivity? There cannot be true objectivity from the inside?*

CP   That is correct. In order to see what a house looks like, you have to step out the door and cross the street.

CD   *That brings me to your statement to Ted Koppel on Night Line. He asked you, "Why didn't you take advantage of the opportunity to have a private visit with the Rebbe?", or something to that*

effect, and your response was that your objectivity would have been
absorbed or swallowed up, I forget the exact word. Did you say you
were scared?

CP   I don't know if I was scared, but if I did use that word all I
meant was that I was concerned about how such a meeting would
affect what I myself want to write about regarding this group. If the
Rebbe were alive today, I still wouldn't want to go see him, and I'll
explain to you why, with the following story.

    A very close friend of mine is one of the great political car-
toonists in the United States. Some months after President Clinton
was elected, he invited a small group of cartoonists to meet with
him in the White House. Clinton is a very charismatic person. He
is, when you see him in person, quite awesome. He's tall, almost
monumental, and gives the impression of being a very real, a very
authentic human being, when you meet him face to face. Now, it is
the business of a political cartoonist to be cool, cynical, and objective. And this political cartoonist told me that it took him months to
restore his objectivity after that meeting, because he was overwhelmed by the personality of Bill Clinton. He really came out of
that meeting with a profound regard for that man. I know of this
dynamic. I've experienced it before with teachers that I've had.

    I didn't want to meet personally with the Rebbe because it
was very clear to me that this was a most unusual human being. I
didn't want to spend 20 minutes or half an hour in a room with him,
and then have to rethink, undo, restructure, my imagination after
that experience. That's all I meant by that.

    A writer does the necessary encountering for his or her
work, and when he feels that his imagination has enough encounter
with the reality that he wants to write about, he walks away from
the reality and lets the imagination work. You don't let the reality
overwhelm the imagination. That's precisely why I didn't want to
see the Rebbe, although Rabbi Shemtov, on many occasions, urged
me to do so, and it would have been very easy to do so.

CD   *So a writer, in a sense, is living in this imaginary world?*

CP   Absolutely. All fiction writers live in an imaginary world, and it's the extent to which the writer permits his or her imagination to be grounded in reality, that you get this rich interface of reality and imagination. Some writers are all imagination. Some writers are more reality than imagination. Every writer has to determine for herself, or himself, this mix is of imagination and reality. Every time I feel that I have enough reality, my imagination will start doing the work. I won't let the reality overwhelm the imagination.

CD   *So the imagination that comes forth at that time is, in a sense, not objective.*

CP   Never is, and nobody is. Even scientists are not objective. We know enough about how science and scientists work to realize that the most we really do with our lives is make pragmatic paradigms or models. We're working out of our own deepest sense of things, every single one of us, trying to create models out of this inundation we call living and experience. We are trying to make it make sense. We're trying to give it meaning. And it's these models that we communicate to one another. If experience becomes overwhelming, and the models don't work, we change the models.

       A very simple example, what's happening in Lubavitch today. Lubavitch had a very coherent model of its nature and the nature of its relationship to the Jewish world and the world at large. At the core of that model was the Rebbe. And for many Lubavitch Chasidism the essential power of that model lay in the possibility that the Rebbe was the Moshiach, literally the Moshiach, not figuratively. When that didn't happen, what you then had occur is what normally occurs when models are subjected to new evidence, to harsh reality. That is to say, the model is reinterpreted, it's reshaped, so you have a different understanding of the message of the Rebbe and of "Messianism," among many Lubavitch Chasidism today.

CD   *Have you seen the Rebbe's impact on the conservative and reform movements?*

CP   No, not really. In terms of political relationship in Jewish life, my sense is that there's very little going on if anything between Lubavitch and conservative, Lubavitch and reform. Indeed, I'm not sure there's much going on between Lubavitch and Yeshiva orthodoxy.

CD   *I want to go back to the 50's and 60's, when the Rebbe had contact with Saul Lieberman, professors Dimetrofsky, Zlotnik, and several people at the seminary. Seems to me there was an interesting dialogue going on.*

CP   There was always personal contact between some great Chasidic leaders and great Rabbonim, from the time of the Baal Shem Tov and on. But that personal contact is very different from contact between the movements. Yoshe Ber Soloveitchik came to visit the Rebbe and the two of them talked. But those interpersonal dialogues have little effect on the Jewish world. My sense of it is that once you pass the generation of the Baal Shem Tov and his immediate followers, who converted rabbis to Chasidism, there is not much that is constructive going on between Chasidism and the Yeshiva world or the worlds of Conservative and Reform Judaism.

But there is another interesting and more subtle effect, and that is that Chasidism, with its sense of joy, its radiant way of approaching G-d through the heart, rather than through the head, which is very much the Yeshiva way, that radiance has really spread through Jewish life. If you see kids dancing in a summer camp today, singing in a certain way, much of that singing and dancing is probably the result of Chasidic influence radiating from the beginnings of Chasidism through the whole body of Judaism. To that extent it is true, there is an influence of Chasidism on the whole body of Jewish life.

But as far as political influence, other than the fact that all of religious Jewish life has shifted to the right since the Holocaust and the Second World War and the creation of the State of Israel, and some of that shifting can be attributed to the renaissance of the Yeshiva world and Chasidism, I do not see any direct movement-to-movement influence.

CD   *Have you actually studied and learned any of the Rebbe's writings?*

CP   I have read two of his teshuvos, responsa. One had to do with Techiyas Hamesim, Resurrection of the Dead, the other had to do with not moving from the neighborhood of Crown Heights. I have read his divrei Torah. I have studied many sections of the Tanya.

CD   *The Tanya you've studied on your own or with someone else?*

CP   On my own. I discussed parts of the Tanya with Rabbi Shemtov, because we used to have long trips together. I remember a discussion with Shemtov about the section in the Tanya having to with the fact that gentiles have no souls. It was a little upsetting to me.

CD   *I can understand that you were upset; however, did you get an explanation from Shemtov?*

CP   His explanation was straightforward.

CD   *It is not that simple, because if a gentile fulfills the seven universal commandments, he does have a portion in the world to come. The Rambam says this. The Tanya is talking about those gentiles that do not fulfill the seven Noachide laws.*
    You mentioned before that the philosophical ideas of Chabad Chasidism are unique. The element of Yesh meAyin. The spreading of the wellsprings.

CP   Uforatzta.

CD   *But that Uforatzta is the result of a deep understanding of Hashem, on a philosophical and intellectual level, that inspires the individual and then there comes the maaseh b'poel, the deed. Do you think that had a lot to do with the Lubavitcher movement?*

CP   Absolutely. There's no question that at the core of the evan-
gelical thrust is a very profound belief that they were doing G-d's
work, and that they were doing it at the command of G-d. It's not
easy to determine what pushed what. It may well be that the rationale came after the realization of the need, rather than the other way
around. But that's perfectly fine. There's nothing wrong with the
then Lubavitcher Rebbe sitting at a table with his staff in 1825 and
looking at what was happening to the Jewish people, and seeing
that the thing to do was to build Yeshivos, and then they develop a
rationale for suddenly starting to evangelize among the whole
Jewish people in Russia. Or perhaps they had the rationale first and
then started to evangelize. I don't think anyone, unless they took
minutes of those meetings, can reconstruct what that dynamic was.
But that they had a profound belief that they were doing G-d's
work, I don't doubt for a minute.

CD   *Which came first, is what you are saying.*

CP   I have never seen a clear picture of which came first and I'm
not at all certain of how, methodologically, you could do it. My
guess is that the theology, as it were, was latent, and was brought
out as a part of the terrible need that suddenly pushed itself forward
in the early years of Nicholas I.

CD   *In studying and reading the Rebbe's works over the years,
have you seen some of his Gadlus, greatness in Torah, in the work
itself?*

CP   I have seen what I would call normal Chasidus in his work,
the very expected use of texts to expound one's particular position.
I have not seen any serious scholarship. I have not seen any sense
of the layers of Jewish history, of the rich complexity of Jewish history and Jewish thought through the centuries. But I never expected to see that. What I expected to see was a profound awareness of
classical texts, a very broad knowledge of Torah and Gemorah. I

saw the Rebbe using Torah for what were essentially his purposes and the purposes of the movement. That's perfectly legitimate. Many use Torah in that way.

CD   *Can Chasidism, in your opinion, be for everyone?*

CP   If by "for everyone," you mean the 50% of Jews who are not interested in anything Jewish, not even in Reform Judaism, then I don't quite see what there is in Chasidism that could be of interest to them other than its singing, dancing, the occasional "feelgood" dvar Torah, and so on.

Can the core of Jewish tradition itself be affected by Chasidism? Well, it has been affected by Chasidism. Can modern Jews and American Jews be transformed totally by Chasidism and by Lubavitch? I doubt it very much. But that does not mean you should not try. You do not want, and I don't want, and nobody wants all of Judaism to become Lubavitch.

CD   *Of course. That I understand. What I'm saying is that a person in Yeshiva University is learning a Gemorah, for it to be a simcha, a real joy in learning a Gemorah and to use it as a way of complementing intellectualism. Shouldn't that be a goal?*

CP   Yes, and it is. For example in Israel, where I lived for 4 years and belonged to an orthodox synagogue, filled with Yeshiva people, when it came Simchas Torah those Yeshiva people were dancing like any Chasid. It's no longer the case that Chasidism have an exclusive hold on joy. To that extent Chasidism has succeeded: My nephew is a Yeshiva ilui, a genius, and he sings and dances also. He teaches Talmud at Yeshiva University. This is no longer a monopoly of Chasidism.

CD   *What do you believe is the Rebbe's everlasting message?*

CP   I think he successfully created a worldwide movement that caught the imagination not only of Jews but also of non-Jews. I think there was a charismatic quality to his being that spilled over beyond the boundaries of Lubavitch and of the Jewish people to the world at large . I think that while it's true that he surrounded himself with very clever staff people who know how to work the media, it's at the same time true that the media would not have taken to him the way they did, were there not something of substance there.

I would be in a distant place, or my children would travel to remote parts of the world, and once people found out that we were from the East coast of the United States, very often, the talk would drift to the Rebbe. I was at a party in Seoul, Korea, for example, just a year or so before the Rebbe passed away, and the American ambassador leaned over to me and said, "I understand that the Lubavitcher Rebbe is very sick." On a mountaintop in Seoul, Korea, we're talking about the Rebbe!

My daughter, was in Ireland a couple or so years ago for a conference on James Joyce. She delivered her paper and then got on her bicycle and went riding all over Ireland. She crossed over to a little island of the coast of Ireland, and was having dinner at an inn, and the owner of the inn came over to her, and they started talking, and the owner said to her in his Irish brogue, "Where are you from?", and she said, "I'm from the East coast of the United States," and he said, "The east coast? Oh? I understand that the Lubavitcher Rebbe is very sick."

That is the kind of thing that happened as a result of the media exposure. But if it were not for the fact that there was content there, the media would not have gone to him so often. From the point of view of his personality, he made a significant contribution to Judaism. From the point of view of his fundamentalism, of certain stands that he took politically, especially vis a vis Israel, he almost succeeded in splitting the Jewish people. So you have this balancing act, and you have to be very honest about the good and the not-so-good when you come to dealing with a very great man. From my own point of view there was greatness, and there were also things that were not so great.

CD   *So, as a writer, does all of the above impact you in your writing?*

CP   Absolutely. Because what you always want to write about is a person who is both great, impacts on people, interacts with the greatest and the most ordinary of people, cares about people, and at the same time is so human that he can make mistakes, worry about his successes, have doubts, question his moves, and from time to time say to those closest to him, "What do you want from me, I'm only a human being." That's a really great man. And that kind of human being is fascinating to a writer to explore.

CD   *What would you say is the difference in the writing of Soloveitchik, as compared to the Rebbe?*

CP   Soloveitchik was aware of, and related to, some of the greatest minds in modern European philosophy. Kierkegaard and others are part of the warp and the woof of Halachic Man, for example. I was his student. He probably knew but was afraid to use technical, text scholarship, which questions the veracity and the solidity of the Biblical text. Torah law is derived from the Biblical text, and if the text isn't solid, you don't know what you're committed to. You have to rethink the core of your Jewish existence. Rabbi Soloveitchik, as I knew him, certainly would not publicly acknowledge that he was rethinking the core of his existence. But I think he knew this modern "Torah".

I have no inkling that the Rebbe really knew the techniques of modern scholarship. If he did, I wish someone would tell me, because this would give me something to write about in a novel! No one that I ever spoke to has given me any inkling that he knew archaeology, philology, philosophy, sociology, the whole complex mechanism that we call modern technical scholarship on classical texts.

CD   *The Rebbe had tremendous academic scholarship. In my interviews with Professor Branover and Rabbi Nissen Mangel it is very obvious that the Rebbe had that wisdom. As you yourself said, "the Rebbe was a different kind of Rebbe," he had to be well versed in all subjects from sociology to anthropology. However, his great-*

ness was his being a Rebbe, the Moshe Rabbeinu of our generation. And as the Moshe of our generation he was able to communicate with every individual, Jew or gentile, on any subject. This position will prove itself when, in the very near future, the Rebbe's personal notes will be printed in the English language. It's currently available in Hebrew in what's called the "Rishimos".

Recently there appeared a new book, selected from the Rebbe's work, called Towards a Meaningful Life. In the book they have the footnotes from a letter discovered from the 1930's dealing with Darwinism, evolution, which shows he was familiar with the sciences. Also, he studied and graduated with Soloveitchik at the Sorbonne, and Berlin. He graduated as an engineer. I'll have to put together a packet for you of some of his writings. Professor Branover told me that the Rebbe was well-versed in the latest scientific discoveries.

As far as your comments about Rabbi Soloveitchik "rethinking his own core existence (as a 'fundamentalist Jew')," I know from all evidence that he was committed to Torah, not just in practice but in spirit, more than one hundred percent.

CP   What I'm waiting for is an account of the Rebbe's personal library, the one in his home. Whether or not there were any books that he marked up — not seforim, Hebrew books, but books in English, German. I have not seen such a list. The next time you see my good friend Avrohom Shemtov, ask him where this list is.

CD   *During the trial of the previous Rebbe's library books, the Rebbe said that his father-in-law had all kinds of books in the library. As a Jewish leader, he needed to have access to all books.*

CP   I understand, but that's my question. What books?

CD   *The Rebbe is not present physically today. What is the direction you think Lubavitch will take?*

CP   The fact that we're sitting here and talking about the Rebbe indicates that his "presence," physical or otherwise, is still among us.

When such a leader dies, and his followers have this degree of commitment to him, one of several things takes place. One is to reinterpret, to delay the Messianism. We have done it, the Christians have done it.

Lubavitch Chasidim are doing it, they're waiting for some future coming.

The second is to come to terms with the grief and mortality and to use whatever presence he has left behind, to build with. You begin to invest your energies in a holding action to keep the movement alive, and at the same time, the antennae go out to see who might be the future leader. Meanwhile, once the center crumbles, if the movement is really strong, then all the different pieces of it will become centers in their own areas. Then you have regionalism. So Hong Kong is strong, Los Angeles is strong, and Crown Heights becomes just another region. Who knows where the next leader will come from? It's in the nature of charisma that it's a mystery. Whoever it is, the process of choosing is fairly obvious. Enough Lubavitchers will have to agree that this individual is charismatic, and they will appoint him a leader. If others disagree, you have a split... Then the new Rebbe will have to spend ten years of his life building upon his successes and his charisma in order to become a major figure.

My sense now is that Lubavitch is in a holding pattern, it is regional, the central committee is operating out of Crown Heights and doing the very best it can to hold things together, that there is more than one voice, and that it's waiting for G-d, to help them and tell them what to do.

It's also my sense that it will come through all this and there will be a new leader in time.

CD *You feel it imperative for the movement to continue, that there be another Rebbe?*

CP I think it would be a disaster if Lubavitch disappears.

CD *Could you see it carrying on without a Rebbe?*

164

CP   I could see it continuing in its regional mode for a good decade, but I think there will be a leader within a decade. He may surprise all of you. Or there may be a fight, or a split, and the movement will regroup and go on.

CD   *Do you believe that the Rebbe could have been, was, Moshiach?*

CP   In the literal sense?

CD   *Yes.*

CP   I don't believe he was Moshiach for the same reason Jews didn't believe that any other individual was Moshiach. The world is not better. It hasn't been redeemed or transformed. He didn't reveal himself.

CD   *Did he have what it took to be a Moshiach?*

CP   I don't know what it takes to be a Moshiach. Some say that the world will be transformed; others say that all the world will recognize G-d and there will be a political transformation — Jews will go to Eretz Yisroel, but there will be no metaphysical transformation. Neither of those things has occurred.

CD   *I'm sure that the section of Lubavitch Chasidim who believe he is Moshiach point to the fact that he said certain things, without actually saying "I am the Moshiach," allude very strongly to that assertion.*

CP   Yes, but one of the essential ingredients of Messiahhood is that there's no ambivalence.

CD   *Rabbi Groner says a woman once came to him and was saying the Rebbe was Moshiach. She was nudging Groner. So he went into the Rebbe and said, "What are you waiting for, reveal your-*

self!" The Rebbe said Moshiach will not know he is Moshiach until the very moment when it will be revealed by Hashem.

CP   That's exactly what I mean. There will be no unclarity about that moment.

CD   *I would like to speak for a moment about* The Chosen. *May I?*

CP   Sure.

CD   *It's clear that you have an affinity for Chasidism, but I get the feeling there's some turmoil, something bothering you, as portrayed by* The Chosen. *It seems to me your heart and soul is there. One hand there is a love for Chasidism and on the other hand you seem to be very uncomfortable with certain acts of Chasidism; that, to use a hard word, you despise some aspects of Chasidism. Is that a correct interpretation?*

CP   Ambivalence is a more correct way of expressing my feelings. I grew up in a Chasidic home and I know the power of Chasidism. What I don't like is its fundamentalism, its inability to come to terms with modernity, its attitude which despises all of modern culture indiscriminately. Yet I understand its power, its radiance. It's that back and forth ambivalence that I try to portray in *The Chosen*, where the issue is with two major elements of secularism — Freudian theory, and socialist secular Zionism. In *Asher Lev* , it's art.

CD   *Where did you get the source for* The Silence*? That hits everyone.*

CP   There is a strain of silence in Chasidism. The Kotzker Rebbe did not speak for about twenty years. There is a strong emphasis on silence in the quotations I have in *The Chosen*, from classic Jewish sources, Gemorah and Kabbalah.

CD   *It seems, from your remarks about Soloveitchik that the ambivalence is not just to Chasidus but to Orthodoxy. Why make the point about silence more by the Chasid than by Soloveitchik and Yeshiva University? Is it because Yeshiva University has a college and gives a degree, that you are more comfortable?*

CP   I deal with intellectual Yeshiva issues in *In the Beginning.* The issue in *My Name Is Asher Lev* has to do with art, and artists, which involves the heart and the imagination. In *The Chosen* I dealt with silence and Freud because both involve the heart and the imagination. Chasidism is about the human heart. When it came to an intellectual problem, I put it into a Yeshiva world.

12

Mr. Yitzchok Shamir
Former Prime Minister State of Israel

ISRAEL'S SECURITY

CD   *Mr. Shamir, please tell a little about yourself and the your association with the Lubavitcher Rebbe. Where were you born and what year did you come to Israel?*

YS   I came here in 1935 from eastern Poland. Now it's Belarus. Vuzhinoy, it was a small shtetel of Misnagdim, not any Chasid was there. It was near Slonim, that area. Now it is White Russia. I visited my shtetel two years ago, but I found nothing. The only part that still exists is a small part of the cemetery. The Goyim were very nice, the Prime Minister gave me the use of a helicopter from Minsk, they escorted me. The last Jew died there five years ago.

I was active in Irgun and in the Lehi movement during the World War, before the war, and after it, until the establishment of the State of Israel. Then I was active in the Mosad for 10 years. I came back, after a short interruption in private business, to join Herut, and then Likud in 1969-70. That began my political career. I was elected to the Knesset, then became Foreign Minister, Prime Minister. I am now a Member of the Knesset but already not very active.

I never met the Rebbe personally. Of course, I've known a lot about him. I have met many people who met him. I was very impressed by all his activities, first by his initiative in starting activities for the rescue of the Soviet Jews. I was personally active in this undertaking, before joining Herut. That was around 1966-67.

After the Six Day War, in the Soviet Union there began to

168

develop various Jewish movements, trying to make Aliyah. The Aliyah began thanks to the Six Day War. I was a member of a group that established contacts with those people active in the underground in Russia. From them I learned that the Rebbe of Chabad sent Shluchim there, before us. Since then I admired him. I saw in him a man who felt the responsibility to be the one who has to take on himself the responsibility to take care of all the Jewish people, everywhere in the world.

I was very sensitive to many critical situations where Jewish people found themselves. It was not important where, or in which conditions. It could be in Russia or in a forgotten small place in an Arab land. He sent Shluchim to help them.

After the war it was well known that the Rebbe took a very strong position on the fate of the territories taken by us in the war. He became the spiritual leader of the whole movement that fought for keeping and not giving up these parts of Eretz Yisroel which came into our possession.

Afterwards, when I became a member of the Herut, then of the Knesset and of the government, we established contact, mainly by letters and oral messages. Many people involved with him came to see me and to bring messages that encouraged me, and convinced me to stay strong and to keep all that we have in Eretz Yisroel, not to give the Arabs what we liberated.

This contact with the Rebbe gave me a lot of strength and courage. I have met many people who have been his Chasidim. If we know that someone is a chasid of the Rebbe, we can count on him that he will always be with us. I saw he was very strongly convinced in his teachings about the faithfulness to Eretz Yisroel, to Yerushalayim. He tried to help us in our political struggle. He was an expert on the political conditions inside Israel. Sometimes he helped us through his contacts with many people of good will, in keeping our government.

We have been attacked and threatened by our rivals, the leftists. I remember one special moment when Mr. Peres, who is now the Foreign Minister, tried to topple my government by getting a majority. He almost got it, but the Rebbe made an effort. He did not give him the possibility to get a majority, because of his influ-

ence on two members of the Knesset. There was constant communication by telephone, and the Rebbe got reports on what is going
on here, and how important is his efforts not to let them take over
the government.

At that time some of the religious parties were very important, they had the force to make a difference.

The crisis began with the decision of the "Shas" people to
leave our government. The Rebbe didn't have an influence on these
people, so he found two men, Rav Werdiger and Mizrachi, and convinced them to stay strong against all the pressures. And there were
pressures on them.

Mr. Peres did not succeed in liquidating our government,
and we continued our activity for more than two years, which was
very important. I felt very strongly the effect of the Rebbe and his
determination to stand with us and to help us in everything. I
remember he sent me one of his men, Rav Gutnick, from Australia,
with instructions to stand by us and help us in keeping contact with
all the religious parties in Israel, and to maintain the unity around
our government, and he was successful.

I got, from time to time letters from the Rebbe, mainly
about these issues of Eretz Yisroel, until we couldn't continue. I
regret this very much. His men continued his work according to his
instructions, but it couldn't have the same strength and the same
impact as it was.

Since then, my relations with the Chabad movement continue. I am very happy to see their people, to help them and be
helped by them in convincing the majority of the Jewish people to
stay by what the Rebbe has said, to keep Eretz Yisroel in its integri-
ty, its entirety.

We are still going on, till this day. I hope that the Chabad
movement will continue to stay strong in this struggle.

CD   *Do you have any letters which the Rebbe sent you in the
earlier years? Did you speak by phone with his secretaries during
your years in the government?*

YS   The letters were very short. It was always in the hands of a

Shliach. I didn't get letters about Russia, but I think the Rebbe knew about my activity there and my admiration for the work of his people there. There have been some calls, not personally by me, but by those who worked with me, Eli Rubinstein and others. They did whatever they could. The Rebbe gave very strong instructions to stand with us all the time.

CD   *What's going to be now?*

YS   It's a very bitter situation now. I never imagined that they would come to such decisions and such actions on the ground. No one imagined they would dare to do such acts against the interests of the people of Israel. Not just against the dreams, the inspirations, the halachos, but even against the daily interests, the security interests of our people here.

There is not anything which could explain these positions. We cannot understand what is the motivation of Rabin and Peres. After all, we have not been defeated Chas VeSholom in war. We have been victorious all the time. We are under absolutely no pressure. We are not compelled to do anything we don't want to do.

I cannot understand what they want!! The Jewish state could be today in the best condition we have ever been in our history. Boruch Hashem, we have a lot of Jewish people. It's not enough, but Boruch Hashem it's the only place in the world where the Jewish people are multiplying. We can go forward. In every sector of life we are making progress, and we can make more progress — in the economy, in military strength, in technology, in Aliyah. We had this massive immigration from Russia, and we could continue, if the government cared.

I cannot understand why the situation is getting worse and worse. We are going to lose the Golan Heights. I don't know why. It's the only strategic stronghold we have in the north of our country. Syria is a bitter, dangerous enemy. It's never said or done anything which might express some change in their attitude. The moment we leave the Golan Heights we will get much weaker. It will be like an invitation to the Syrians to come and invade us. They will come, they will get the shores of the Kinneret.

171

As far as Yehuda and Shomron, and Gaza, they are the cradle of our people. Hebron and all the other places. Why do we have to leave? We can develop more and more and more. It's a miracle that we have there Jewish people, wonderful people, who are ready to sacrifice themselves, to live and work and stay against all the dangers and threats.

Then there is Yerushalayim. When I was Prime Minister, no one even imagined that one day we would lose a part of Jerusalem. Now, first of all Mr. Rabin permitted the Arab residents of Jerusalem to participate in the autonomy elections. We were always against this. For us Yerushalayim was not a part of Yehuda and Shomron. We said that it was a national concern that all of Jerusalem should be under the control of the State of Israel.

Rabin and Peres are still saying the same thing, but their actions are the opposite. They have given them permission to participate in their elections. Now there are special negotiations with the Arabs about "the fate of Jerusalem." We never agreed to such things. Our position, and Begin's position, was that we have nothing to negotiate. This is our capital.

Now, when in the United States there is an influential group in the Senate that wants to bring the American Embassy from Tel Aviv to Jerusalem, our government is against it, because Arafat is against it.

We could not imagine this! Since the beginning of the State, it was the dream of all the Israeli governments, that one day America would recognize our rights in Jerusalem and agree that their embassy, like the embassy in all countries, will be in the capital. If America does it, all the other countries will follow. With such an opportunity, they are against it, because Arafat is against it. This means that Arafat dictates our policy!

What we did in the Oslo agreements was the reason, the real reason, for many terrorist acts by the Arabs, acts that succeeded in killing tens of Jewish people. After the control of the security of Gaza was given to the Arabs, they made use of it. They have organized in Gaza many terrorist acts that were carried out in other places, Yerushalayim, Tel Aviv. Gaza was the center!!

Now, after three months of quiet, they want to give up security arrangements to the Arabs in all the other cities of Yehuda and Shomron, Bet Lechem and Ramallah, and Tulkarem, Jenin, Kalkilia, and so on. The same thing that happened in Gaza will happen in Yehuda and Shomron. It will be a real danger to the existence of our people, not only of the mitnachalim [settlers] who live there, but everyone.

Until now all the countries of the world respected us. They know Israel is strong. Now they are watching carefully, they are not doing anything, but they are waiting till we give these parts of the land back to the Arabs, then all these countries will feel safe that Israel will not be able to change the situation.

I hope they will not succeed in all this before the elections in November 1996, which is more than a year. If they lose, it could of course be an opportunity to save the land of Israel, the people of Israel. Chabad is not a mass movement. You don't have millions. But I think thanks to the spirit of the Rebbe you have a great amount of energy, and I see you are able to do many things.

For example, a few days ago I was in Paris, and the people who were on the side of Likud, together with the Chabad people in Paris, organized a great demonstration for Yerushalayim, and to celebrate an anniversary of the educational work of Chabad in Paris. They have a big school there. They have done something important for the education of the Jewish Youth.

They invited me to participate, and a large crowd came to this demonstration, 15,000 people. Paris is not New York. The Chabad people, the Likud people, many Jewish people. It was a very impressive demonstration. You know there Rabbi Pewsner, I was in their synagogue. I spoke. It's nice, it's Yiddishkeit.

We have to work together. Of course I hope that you become stronger and stronger. I do not know how it will happen without the Rebbe, but...

CD   *You said earlier that the people of Israel are basically against what Rabin and Peres are trying to do. I was on a plane a year ago back from Eretz Yisroel, and I asked the person sitting next to me. He said at least 50% of the country supports their giving back of territory.*

YS   I do not know exactly. Such things cannot be known precisely without elections. They are the test, but we have to work
before the elections.

CD   *Have you seen the Rebbe's Shluchim throughout the country?*

YS   We meet from time to time. The last time in America I spent
a day in Columbus, Ohio. I met there by accident Rav Krinsky, who
had been invited by the Schottenstein family. When I was in Miami
I met there also a Shliach, Sholom Ber Lipskar. I visited his shul.
He is a very strong personality. You have good people in many
places. I trust you are getting more

CD   *One of the arguments of the Labor government is that they
want to make Israel the Switzerland of the Middle East. Aside from
giving up the land, what is the politically wrong with that idea?*

YS   Ay [krechtz] Narrishkeiten, nonsense. Speaking pragmati-
cally, they have said our economy will get a lot of profit. At this
moment we have seen nothing, because our economy is based on
cooperation with the Western countries, America, Europe, even the
Far East. With the Arabs, nothing. It is three years already since the
Oslo conference, and we see nothing. The attitude of the Arab
countries, Syria, the Palestinians has not changed. There are now
investments in the country of Jewish people, some others too, but
no Arabs. When we try to speak with them about business, they
shout, "Now you want to dominate us economically!" they don't
trust us. Therefore we cannot trust them. They are enemies, enemies in blood. This is very deep. You can't discuss anything with
them.

CD   *What about the Jordanians?*

YS   The king is a bit more polite, but the country is very weak
in the area. It has no support from anybody. The Arabs don't like

him, the Egyptians hate him, the Saudis hate him. He doesn't have any friends. He depends for his existence only on us. Therefore he is more polite, but he will never say a word that the other Arabs don't say.

All the others, the PLO say they want Jerusalem to be the capital of the Palestinian state. Their representative in Jerusalem, Faisal Husseini, a nephew of the pogromchik Abd El Kader Husseini, who fought against us in 1948, and was killed by us, and this man is now the representative in Jerusalem of Arafat. He said a few days ago, "What we want is to come back to the situation (in Jerusalem) as it was before 1967." Of course, since then there has been built around Jerusalem housing for 200,000 Jews. Does he want to remove them?

Now Arafat has decided to divide the city of Jerusalem, to establish in the eastern part an Arab municipality of Jerusalem, and our government doesn't say a word. They say of course it's nothing, but they don't even protest. They could have said to Arafat that if he speaks about Jerusalem as the capital of his country, they will stop the negotiations. After all, the Palestinians depend on us, not we on them.

Nothing, nothing. It is clear that if they continue their government, they will give up Jerusalem. I don't know how we will be able to exist. Of course in such a situation Aliyah will not come. The massive Aliyah started after the Six Day War, when Jews got courage. We were strong! It was in the time of Khrushchev, of Brezhnev, and the Russians wrote letters to them that they wanted to go to Israel, Israel is our country, not Russia.

If we will be weak, who will dare to speak in this way? And this applies also to all other countries. It is sad, very sad. What the Labor Party wants, their only motivation is to stay in power. They think that if they continue the negotiations with the Arabs, they will keep quiet one more day at a time, there will not be terror.

And [since] Jews prefer a quiet life, they are confident that the people will accept it and they will continue being in power. This is the whole story.

Yesterday Rabin said he has his doubts if the Palestinians will work together with us. Nu, he has his doubts! What are the conclusions? Nothing!

On the other hand, Peres is very strong in his convictions that territory is not important. The main thing is that these Arabs are not fundamentalists, because our only enemies are the fundamentalists. This is silly. The Syrians are not fundamentalists, but they are very strong against us. The Iraqis who sent the scuds are not fundamentalists. They are friends of ours? They are ready at any moment to send new scuds.

I have the impression that something happened to the spirits of these people, to their equilibrium, because it's unbelievable. You can't imagine what they are thinking, what they are doing. I can understand it's important to them to be in power, but this is more important than the fate of Eretz Yisroel, of the Jewish people?

I don't believe they will succeed with all this. They say they need the approval of the world. The world was not against us! During my premiership the world respected us. With Bush we had some clashes, with the loan, but he was the only one. Since the Six Day War they started to respect us, to see in us a strong factor in the area. We have developed strategic cooperation that has been very important up to this day.

When they see that we are giving up all our strongholds, we are capitulating, they will lose this respect. After all, they are flesh and blood. They have their assessment of their self-interest, and no one wants to be partners with weaklings, nobody.

When I was prime minister, in spite of all these declarations about Palestinian freedom by all these countries, they decided to establish normal ties and do business with us. China, India, the African countries, Spain and so on. Now... Of course, for the other nations it is easier to see that we are less strong, that our positions are weak on Jerusalem. Of course, for the Christians it is better that Jerusalem not be the capital of the Jewish state, but when we are strong they accept it.

This was always the position of the Rebbe. You have to be strong, and then they will respect you. It's logic.

CD *You said before America does not pressure. I remember Christopher was pressuring. Bush was using the loans as a means to get Israel to do what America wants.*

YS   This is pressure? For America, it is convenient for them to make a ceremony on the lawn of the White House. It gives some credit to President Clinton, it could help him in his re-election, but it's not so important that it could change the character of the relationship with us. These loans are nonsense. No more. It was unique to Bush, Bush knows, and anyway he is convinced that because of it he lost the presidency. He says it everywhere. He says he lost because the Jews decided to vote against him, and they have great influence. The other presidents have never dared to make such pressures. Carter is not a friend of us, and we had some conflicts with him. In the first year after "Camp David", he told us, "We have some difference of views, but I will never make use of economic and security assistance to enforce my opinions." He kept his promise. Even at the most strained times he never threatened us in these things.

    Bush was the first. He was an exception because he did not like us. He decided that the Arabs are right. Secretary Baker told me, "the President is convinced that the Arabs are right and you are wrong. These territories belong to them." He couldn't give me an explanation why. Clinton, he is all right. He is supporting the government. He cannot be more Israeli than the Israelis themselves!

CD   *When the Scuds were falling, it seemed like Israel was sitting back.*

YS   We had decided that in such a situation, where the Americans are fighting very seriously against the Iraqis, and there was no doubt about the victory — only that it might take a few days more or less, and on the other hand the Arabs might leave Bush's coalition. Why should we be responsible for breaking the coalition and endangering the victory against Iraq?

    I think we were right. There was a little damage — of course every Jew is indispensible —but there was no alternative. I told Bush that I was against this because we want to defend ourselves, but in this situation, if something happens to us we will consult him.

He realized that my saying we would consult him did not mean we would listen in all cases. We consulted, and we decided as we decided. It turned out good for everyone. After this crisis everybody respected us. I visited in America and in Europe, and people called me a great statesman. We were respected. It was no justification to get into a clash with the United States, considering they fought our enemy. Let us hope for true peace. Not like the false prophets in the book of Jeremiah, "Peace, peace and there is no peace." What we have now, is not peace. Not that you can trust what the Arabs say, but they never say themselves that there will be peace. Their chutzpah is growing from day to day.

CD   *Arafat himself. How did he get this prominence?*

YS   Thanks to us, to Rabin and Peres. They gave him the power. They gave him arms and money, and thanks to us he's getting arms and money from America and everywhere else. They do not have a dollar that does not come from us, and they have the Chutzpah to tell us we have to give up what we got in '67, up to the last centimeter. It's terrible. It has no logic. I don't believe it can continue.

CD   *Does the Likud have any plan to counter this?*

YS   The only plan is to change the situation via elections. We cannot allow ourselves to use violence —- we will not raise our hand against Jewish people. This is worse than all the other things. It will not be useful, on the contrary.

CD   *You have the Rebbe's brochos. I have heard the Rebbe speak many times about how we cannot give back a speck of land.*

YS   This was not only the word of a great man. It was logic. Sechel HaYashar [straight thinking].

13

Dr. Abraham Twerski

Rabbi, Psychiatrist, founder and director of Gateway Rehabilitation Center

RECOVERY AND TORAH

CD   *A little about your contact and relationship with the Rebbe. The Previous Rebbe?*

RT   I was by this Rebbe several times, relatively short visits. The first time was when I was a resident in Psychiatry, at which time the Rebbe strongly urged me to move to New York after I finished.

CD   *Where were you doing the residence?*

RT   In Pittsburgh. He said there were many problems for which a psychiatrist was needed for people who were Bnai Torah, and there was danger in sending them to secular psychiatrists, and my services would be sorely needed in New York. I told the Rebbe that I could not see myself surviving as a unique being. To be the only person to turn to in a city like New York would have been crushing. No day, no night, no Shabbos, no Yom Tov, no nothing.
    The Rebbe sort of smiled, then he agreed...
    That was around 1961 or 1962. Several times I met the Rebbe very, very briefly. The Rebbe send me in a proposal to work on a system of meditation that would be applicable for Bnai Torah. He sent me a paper on meditation in English in which he crossed out parts that he thought were inappropriate, and had written his own comments in the margins, and asked me to develop it. Unfortunately, I was never into meditation, and I kept on putting it

off. When I started to look around for it, I wasn't able to find it. I remember that the parts which were crossed out as inappropriate had to do with the secular and oriental forms of meditation. He saved the good things, taking out what was good [in the paper], and his comments had to do with what to substitute for the omissions, etc., but unfortunately I lost it.

CD   *You mentioned that you never had an interest in meditation as a field. Could you explain why?*

RT   The truth is that I'm not far from it, because many years I worked quite intensively treating patients with hypnosis, and had phenomenal results. As my time got more involved in treating alcoholics and addicts, I essentially left general psychiatry, and I didn't do anything more with hypnosis.

Hypnosis and meditation are quite close. What I still now do is a kind of meditation or self-hypnosis, not having anything to do with the oriental techniques. These are relaxation exercises, and I'm fortunate to be able to go into a kind of trance, and take myself back in time to relive very pleasant scenes of childhood.

It's very fascinating. It beats valium, because it doesn't interfere with the function of the brain. I'll slip back in an easy chair, close my eyes, and allow myself to drift back in time. I'll go back to age 10 and see myself in the country, and for ten or fifteen minutes allow myself to relive the experiences of swimming and playing ball, playing monopoly, reading piles of comic books, all the fun things we did as kids.

I do this a few times a week. It is a kind of meditation, but different than disassociating myself from the world and becoming absorbed in whatever, which I understand has something to do with the other meditation. It is a kind of meditation though, and I strongly advocate it. If I find the other paper on meditation I may very well try to adapt it, do something with it.

CD   *Is there a point of contact between traditional chasidic meditation and what you do?*

RT   Once I get into this I'll take a closer look at the various traditional forms of concentration and meditation. My guess is that they're quite close, but sometimes in things that are close, the difference between Gehenim and Gan Eden is a hair's breadth. There can be a very small distinction between what is appropriate and what can be misleading. If I did anything in this field I would take great caution, run it before some of the authoritative Torah scholars.

I want to tell you something which does not have to do with me personally. When people used to go from Pittsburgh to the Rebbe, especially to receive sweet cake on Hoshanah Rabbah, they would come back and tell me that they requested an extra piece of cake for Dr. Twerski. The Rebbe would give them the extra piece. They walked away, and then the Rebbe would call them back and give them another piece, saying, "and this is for Rabbi Twerski. That's by the way.

I went to the Rebbe a number of times to get dollars for tzedaka and then I think I realized what was behind that. I come across the dollar sometimes. I'm going to put it away of course, and I say to myself, "The Rebbe gave me this dollar to give charity. But if I give charity, then I lose the Rebbe's dollar." So I give a different dollar to charity, to exchange it. One dollar of the Rebbe's I think I've exchanged a hundred times. I think that may have been his intention.

CD   *You go back to the Cherkasser Dynasty?*

RT   Our dynasty goes back to the Cherkasser, then to the Mitteler Rebbe. Of course, the Cherkasser had two years after his wedding where his father-in-law, the Alter Rebbe, supported his learning.

CD   *Do you possess any family traditions concerning the succession of the Chabad Dynasty, that is, the question between the Mitteler Rebbe and Reb Aron of Staroselye after the passing of the Alter Rebbe?*

RT   Reb Aron's writings are very dear to us, we learn their chasidus, but there is no question that the chain follows the Mitteler Rebbe.

I'll tell you an interesting story that I don't know how many people know. It came down to us in the family. It's an indication of how sensitive you have to be in the service of Hashem.

The Cherkasser was a young man when he was supported by the Alter Rebbe, maybe 16 when he was married, whatever. At one time, the Alter Rebbe was going to say a chasidic discourse, so he sat the Cherkasser at his right hand. Before I continue with this story let me tell you another story how the Alter Rebbe chose him as his son-in-law.

This is a story of Reb Boruch of Mezibuz who came to the Chernobler Magid, and said he needed a match for his daughter. The Chernobler Magid said that the boys were asleep, and that he should go in and take a look. Rabbi Boruch walked through and placed his hand on each boy's forehead. When he came to the Cherkasser he stopped and said, "Oy, this is a warm little head! This one is for me." The Chernobler Magid told him, "The Litvak (Alter Rebbe) has already grabbed him." A famous story.

Getting back to the first story, the Alter Rebbe was about to say this discourse, and sat the Cherkasser at his Right hand. After he finished he asked him to repeat it back to him. The Cherkasser said "I didn't hear." The Alter Rebbe said, "Weren't you sitting here?" He said, "What I don't have permission to hear I don't hear." The Alter Rebbe told him to go back to Chernobyl and ask his father for permission to receive from him. He left and came back with permission. You can see from what little is left of the Cherkasser's writings that it totally resembles the Alter Rebbe's Likutei Torah. You see that he was heavily influenced, but the lesson is, "What could have gone wrong had he listened to the Alter Rebbe?" The answer is that by these spiritual giants, if there are two paths in the service of Hashem, both completely holy, holy of holies, nevertheless to change one for another cannot be done without permission. It's not a play-toy. You don't do things just because you want to.

CD   *In many of your books you write about your father. I under-stand he was a Rebbe. Did he have a relationship with the earlier leaders of Lubavitch?*

RT   I couldn't tell you. Correspondence I'm not aware of. There couldn't have been much of a relationship because he came to the United States as a young man. I don't think he as 30 yet. I know he was by the Previous Rebbe several times in New York. One inter-esting thing. My oldest brother, of blessed memory, was thinking of going to college. Back around 1942 it was considered a radical move for a Chasidishe Bochur to go to college. He went in to the Previous Rebbe to ask. He heard him out and said, "Do you have a father?" That was the answer, do what your father tells you.

It reminds me of a similar story. The family custom is that girls begin lighting Shabbos Candles at Bas Mitzvah, and the light two candles. When my granddaughter was nine year old and all the girls in her class were lighting Shabbos Candles, and she asked me what to do. I said, "Why don't you write to the Rebbe and ask him." She sat down, with a little bit of help she wrote a letter in English, "Dear Rebbe, all the girls in my class light Shabbos Candles, and my father says that in our family, girls wait until they are 12. What should I do?"

Sometimes you had to wait weeks for an answer. Two days later, here's a letter. The Rebbe answered in Hebrew, "There is no question here. [It is proper] to listen to the grandfather." I saw that she wanted to light Shabbos Candles like the other kids, so I told her to go ahead!

CD   *I understand you used to give a class in Tanya. In your work, do you find the insight of the Tanya applicable for psychia-trists, psychologists, other people in mental health?*

RT   I gave this class before morning prayers and it's all on tape, but it's a very poor quality tape. That was the first time I gave a class in Tanya. G-d willing, I'll do another series with better recording. There were insights into Tanya we were able to get. Of course there are other commentaries. There is the Rebbe's commentary, you have Adin Steinsalz, but still, every time you approach it you get new insights.

The Tanya is very much applicable to all. The first thing is that psychiatry and psychology have a very narrow outlook. Mental health professionals have taken the position that a person's religious, spiritual life is out of their area. They don't deal with it. That's at least halfway decent. The psychoanalytic people used to regularly attack religion. Now it's more neutral, but what they don't realize is that just as there are essential vitamins, and without them there are symptoms of a deficiency disease, there are essential vitamins for the soul.

What a person needs to realize is that he has a soul, that's number one, and this applies to a Non-Jew as well. There is a soul, and the soul has a purpose given to it by its Creator. If we don't apply this nutrition, the Torah being food for the soul, as explained in chasidus, then there is going to be a deficiency syndrome. The symptom is that the individual will feel ill-at-ease and not know what he's missing. The problem is that when you don't know what you are missing you go for all kinds of things. [A person can say to himself that] maybe food will help him feel better, maybe drugs, alcohol, money, pride, ego, whatever. It's a bottomless pit, because they're neglecting the fact that there is something which the soul needs.

My feeling is that the psychologist or psychotherapist needs to be able to simply confidently tell someone that they have definite spiritual nutritional needs. Not to impose one's own perspectives on the client, but to make him aware that he has to deal with these needs. One thing that has been very easy for me to do is working with the alcoholic, because there it is recognized, and stated very clearly in the program of Alcoholics Anonymous, that the problem is that physical needs were placed before spiritual needs. There, the key realization is that one has fallen into this bottomless pit through neglecting spiritual needs.

For the Jew, who has a Neshomah and who has to be supplied with the spiritual needs of the Neshomah, of course the Tanya's approach is significant. If one says he favors a Musar approach, OK. If you really take a look at it "These and these are

184

the words of the living G-d", they're saying the same using different words. Yes, there are some fine differences.

I do use the things I learn from Tanya in working with clients, especially what is so important, the concept theat the brain rules over the heart. We're living in the king of culture where it's the reverse, the emotions are everything. We live by emotions, and Freud said the whole business of behavior is a question of which emotion is going to win out, a conflict of emotions. No one bothers to deal with the fact that the intellect is, or should be, dominant over the emotions. This concept is very important in helping guide people. Not that I have to tell people what there brain should tell them. I can leave them the freedom to decide. They have to realize that it's the brain. They've got to put the brain to use because everything else goes with emotions.

CD   *If someone is chemically dependent, does it help to tell him these things when you really have to deal with the chemical dependency?*

RT   You have to deal with the chemical dependency first, because as long as a brain is doused in either alcohol or any of the other drugs there's no talking to it. First you have to get the individual chemically free. After he is chemically free then you have to start building up some kind of spiritual structure. And it works!

CD   *Of course you know that I deal with psychologists and counselors. Initially they are very doubtful about neshomah, spiritual things. They respond, "This is a chemical issue."*

RT   Are you referring to counselors in chemical dependency fields?

CD   *No.*

RT   Well, we may be talking about biochemical diseases. That's something else. Biochemical diseases are primarily depressive, where there seems to be no question at all that in some people something has gone haywire with their biochemistry. In those situations they have to have correction with the medication. But, what happens is that the medication hopefully restores that to normal, and takes care of the first kind of depression. There are two types of depression, one that is not biochemical, which is due to lifelong dissatisfactions, a kind of grief reaction. Here medication won't help. Medications only help for the type that is due to a biochemical quirk. In these situations you need the correction of medication so the individual will become normal. But then you're dealing with a normal person who has needs for spiritual nutrition.

CD   *I heard a tape of a lecture you gave at the Nefesh conference in Florida this past December. You spoke about anger. The Alter Rebbe also speaks about anger, in Tanya. Do I understand you correctly that the initial impulse, the reflex of anger, that's not within the human beings control?*

RT   You have to get the whole context of the thing. Usually anger is a reflex — the feeling of anger is not within the individual's control. What is within the individual's control is how he reacts to the anger, and where he keeps it, or tries to keep it. However, even though it is not within the individual's control, a person has the capacity to ask Hashem to relieve him of it, and if he feels that it is a severe annoyance and a severe hindrance, then he can ask Hashem to relieve him of it. Also, Hashem's response may very well be, "You haven't done your homework yet. I'm not going to intervene until you first do your thing. You first see to get rid of all the anger that you can. You work on that — you work on your character, to not react, your quality of humility that you shouldn't feel so offended if your honor was hurt. You do your thing.

"Now, after you've done your homework and you're still bothered by it, then come to me." If you're going to say, "No, I'm not going to do anything. I don't like this anger — You get rid of it for me," Hashem is going to say, "No way. You do your homework first. That's part of the Avodah [Process of Divine Service]." It may well be that for reasons known to Hashem He wants us to continue to work on it. What I said was, that without Siyata Dishmaya [Divine help], just by normal human action, a person has no control over the reflex, initial feeling of anger. But if he does the right thing, and asks for Hashem's kindness to remove it, it can be done.

CD   *And this holds equally for a Jew and a gentile?*

RT   The same would be true for a Jew and a gentile. A gentile can develop some very beautiful character qualities. For instance, the Tanach teaches us how King Solomon prayed that the gentiles would also be able to come to the Temple and that their prayers and sacrifices should be accepted. So a gentile also has access to Hashem's Kindnesses.

CD   *The conceptual point about anger which is developed in the Tanya is the saying of our Sages, "Everyone who gets angry is like he is serving idols."*

RT   What I said in my speech in Florida was that the Hebrew word for anger, Kaas, is one word that has three applications. It stands for the first reflex action, the retained anger, and the re-action to it. It can mean any of these three. As far as the actual wording of this saying Maimonides says "Anyone who gets angry", which is the expression of the Zohar. The Talmud has the saying, "Anyone who breaks things out of rage."

In order to reconcile these two sayings, not to assume a difference of opinion without overwhelming evidence, it's logical to say that the Zohar is talking about the same thing as the Talmud, an anger which is expressed. If you're going to say that just because someone feels angry, that's idol worship, that's not the sense in which the word is used. That interpretation I cannot accept. The meaning is that if after he hits me in the face I go and pick up a chair and hit him over the head, that's the anger that the Talmud is talking about and I think that's what the Zohar and Maimonides are saying. It's the final phase of anger, the reaction.

CD   *I'd like to go back to the Chasidic ideas of Cherkass. Is it more an intellectual or an emotional type of Chasidus? Is it in line with the intellectual Chabad Chasidus of the Alter Rebbe?*

RT   They're in line as far as the emotions are concerned, and no one argues abut that. My grandfather, in Pele Yoetz , says that the problem of our generation, this is 110, 120 years ago, is that the intellect does not influence and control the emotions. It's so true of our generation. The intellectual knowledge we've had surpasses anything that's ever happened before, and people's emotional character has not changed. The Alter Rebbe's influence, of course, is on the "three primaries", the qualities of Wisdom, Understanding and Knowledge [symbolized by the acronym Chabad].

The question is whether the approach of the Alter Rebbe is all right for everyone in general? Is it necessary to start with the intellect before working on the emotions? The Alter Rebbe clearly says that that's the way it has to go. What were the feelings of the others, the Polish Rebbe's. Some of them felt that this kind of intellectual work was not in everyone's ability. Others thought it was not good to indulge too much in intellectual investigation of the Divine because it's too close to philosophy and speculation, which can lead a person out of Judaism entirely. They believed in acceptance of guidance and practical character-building without the intellectual depth of the Chabad School.

They are two different paths in the service of Hashem. It's implicit in the story I mentioned about the Cherkasser. He didn't have permission to go from one to the other. But both are "the words of the living G-d."

CD   *What I'm really asking is if the Cherkasser's path was the same as the other Rebbes of Poland, or to the Alter Rebbe.*

RT   The Cherkasser himself was much closer to the Alter Rebbe.

CD   *Today, is there such a thing as Cherkasser chasidus and Chasidim?*

RT   In the last generation there were still Hornstopler Chasidim (who come from the Cherkasser). Today there are remnants, what people tried to hold together. Many times today Chasidus is similarly the strengthening of a bond between people to continue to uphold their tradition practices, that help as a defense against the enormous moral and cultural corruption which is happening. That's what I see of chasidus today.

Chabad still retains learning chasidus in a strong way. Other types of chasidus haven't. They'll look into chasidic books, which is very fine, but they haven't made it a curriculum as has Chabad.

CD   *That's something that has always bothered me. I don't understand it. Shouldn't chasidus be learned?*

RT   They learn chasidus, but what happens is that the average Chasid, not a Chabadnik, will take Siduro Shel Shabbos and learn it. It's gorgeous stuff. He'll take a Bnei Yisoschor, an Or Hamayim, a Kedushas Levi. He'll learn Chasidus, but not as a formal course as Chabad has developed it. Would it have been better otherwise? I think so. I don't know why it didn't develop.

We have a young man, a Chabad Chasid, who comes over every Shabbos. We learn works of Chasidus, Siduro Shel Shabbos and these other works. I pointed out to him that he has his regular learning in Chabad. We have our study, but it's not as organized. However, my great grandfather from Hornistopol, in a [since published] letter to my grandfather, writes that he should know Tanya from beginning to end. Tanya is the absolute foundation of everything.

CD   *Is it true that when people want to sit in your class in Tanya they have to go to the Mikvah first?*

RT   For Tanya you have to go to the Mikvah first. It's a known thing that Zohar can't be learned without Mikvah. I felt that this should be for Tanya also. Just as an example, I'd like to tell you some of the interesting insights that came up. The Alter Rebbe talks about [Chochmah and Binah] Wisdom and Understanding.

Wisdom is the lightning bolt of insight, and Understanding is then the organizing force which develops this insight.

Generally, it's pointed out that Wisdom itself is very difficult to identify, because almost the moment it comes in it's organized into Understanding, and we have very little grasp of Wisdom itself. This is almost impossible to describe on tape, but maybe once I describe it you will get the hang of it. In medical practice, when we see a patient at the bedside, and suspect there is a problem with the brain, a tumor or anything else which may be responsible for his symptoms, the question is how to test? There are various ways of testing, reflexes, etc. There is also a test for stereognosis.

Let me show you. Close your eyes for a moment. I'm going to put something in your hand. Tell me what it is.

CD   *It's a coin.*

RT   You want to tell me a little more?

CD   *It's a quarter.*

RT   The minute you felt this, you felt it was a coin. I have given this to a patient and gotten the answer, "It's hard..., and flat..., and it's round."

I say, "Well, what is it?"

He responds, "It's hard and it's flat and it's round."

He describes what he fells, but he is unable to take the sensations and organize them into a coin because that part of his brain has been interfered with.

When you felt it, you didn't think, "It's hard and flat and round, therefore it is a coin." That didn't even occur to you. Right away, instantaneously, you said, "It is a coin." However, before you were able to conclude that it is a coin, your mind had to process that it's hard and flat and round, therefore it is a coin.

CD   *How do we know that? Do we have proof?*

RT   The proof is that if there is a lesion in one part of the brain you never go beyond that. This means that the initial sensation is the component parts. Then the mind puts them together and organizes them. That's Wisdom and Understanding. Wisdom is the initial impression and Understanding puts them together. The Zohar calls them "Two friends that never separate." They never separate unless a person has a brain tumor. I put a key in a person's hand, he'll say that it's a key. If he has this type of tumor he'll say, "It's hard, it's got a long thing, a little edge is rough."

If I say again, "What is it," he'll again give me the component parts. This behavior is called astereognosis. He is unable to take the individual facts and put them together.

The same thing happens in the process of thought [Machshovoh]. We get inputs from Wisdom and Understanding, but they are two friends that never separate because the moment we get these impressions we translate and organize them with Understanding. We don't even perceive the Wisdom, but actually it precedes the Understanding, and if it were possible to separate them we would see the component parts.

When I gave this explanation in my class everyone understood it with a totally different insight. At times psychologists and psychiatrists attended the class. They understood extremely well what the Alter Rebbe was talking about as pertaining to the different levels of the brain. There are things that go on in the conscious mind, things in the unconscious, and the various level of the preconscious.

The preconscious is something that is never thought about. Right now I am conscious of the fact that I am talking with you. If you were to ask me something that happened many years ago, that's someplace hidden in my brain, I don't remember it. It could come out under hypnosis, or in a dream. Where is it? It's in the unconscious. It's not accessible. However, if you asked me what I did two days ago in San Francisco, I'll think a moment and I'll tell you. That thought is neither in my conscious mind, since I wasn't thinking about it at the time, nor in the unconscious, because it is accessible, so it is in the preconscious

Within the preconscious there are levels. The important

191

thing about this is to understand what the Alter Rebbe means by [the major classifications of spiritual stature which are mentioned in the first chapter of Tanya], Tzaddik vetov lo, Tzaddik vera lo, and Benoni; a complete Tzaddik, an incomplete Tzaddik, and an intermediate person. Without that it's very difficult to understand. A complete Tzaddik has no evil even in the unconscious. It's been totally transformed [to good]. The intermediate person, the Benoni, has no evil in the conscious. The incomplete Tzaddik has no evil in the conscious, no evil in the preconscious, but he has evil in the unconscious.

When we analyze it this way, people understood things they never had before. Psychologists, who work with these concepts, have an idea of how there can be so many levels of Tzaddikim because there are many levels of unconscious and preconscious.

CD   *I'd like to ask you about the Teshuvah movement in America as of 1996. Are you involved with it?*

RT   Tangentially. My brother has been much more assertive. I have not been militantly assertive. Whenever I have an opportunity and people ask me, I'm glad to, but I have reasons of my own.

CD   *Looking at the Rebbe's work over the last 45 years, where are we at? Are we making any progress against assimilation? Where are we going?*

RT   It seems that there's a very sharp dichotomy that's coming through. Unfortunately there is a strong, strong assimilatory force, but more than ever there have been people coming back. The kiruv movement has been very successful and could be even more successful with additional effort.

CD   *What do you think it's lacking?*

RT   I've envisioned the 613 mitzvos as being 613 building blocks for the structure, and that without the 613 building blocks nothing can be done. I've also had the feeling that if you have the

613 blocks and you don't put something together, then all you've got is a pile of bricks. You don't have a house.

I think Chasidus for example has given a structure — this is what you do with Torah and Mitzvos. But first off you've got to have Torah and Mitzvos — without that you have nothing. What's lacking is that people may be turned on to Torah and Mitzvos, thinking it will give them a way of life. After a while some find their way, and others say, "I've been doing this for two years and I don't find that it has been doing anything for me."

For some, Torah and Mitzvos has not been enough, because we have not given them the full structure of Torah and Mitzvos. That's one of the reasons that I made a commentary on The Path of the Just. The statement on which it is based, the Baraisa of Rav Pinchas ben Yair, is a ten-step moral progression all the way from Carefulness to the revelation of the Divine Presence. It does not concern itself with particular Mitzvos.

All correct roads lead to the same goal. The ten steps lead to the same goal as Chasidus has. I think what we need today in Kiruv is to go beyond the keeping of Torah and Mitzvos to such things as Chasidus or Musar teaches. If that doesn't happen you'll have a lot of people who will taste it, because they are looking for something. If they don't go beyond the building building blocks into the structure itself they are going to drop off.

CD   *You are implying that one should search for the Neshomah of the Torah. What made you translate Mesilas Yesharim [The path of the Just]?*

RT   It is very well organized. It goes by gradation from one step to another. It's universally acclaimed. The Mezritcher Magid said that he (the author of Mesilas Yesharim, Rabbi Moshe Chaim Luzzato) died young because his generation did not deserve him. Rabbi Yisroel Salant said that he could compose no end of [Talmudic analysis similar to] the Noda Biyehudah but he could not write one page of the Path of the Just. He is very clear, but I felt there was a need for some clarification and expansion of his ideas.

CD *Do you find a Chasidic warmth in his words?*

RT There sure can be, if you learn it right. The author himself states that this is not a book to be looked at one time, because he is not saying anything new. He's telling you what you know, but what you forget. In a sense that's what the Alter Rebbe does in the Tanya. Tanya begins with the verse that "For the thing is very close to you, in your mouth and heart to do it." That's something everyone knows. What do we do with our knowledge of that? Nothing! We know it and we don't do anything about it. Therefore, just as the Path of the Just has to be reviewed again and again, as he says in the introduction, the same thing is with Tanya. If you learn Tanya once and put it away and say, "I learned it already," nothing has been accomplished. Tanya has to be learned again and again.

I translated The Path of the Just first because it was much simpler and easier, and with Hashem's help we'll do the next one on Tanya.

14

Rabbi Herbert Weiner

Rabbi Emeritus Temple Sharey Tefilo-Israel, New Jersey
and Author of 9 1/2 Mystics

DISGUISED AS A REFORM RABBI

CD   *Rabbi Weiner, several years ago the Rebbe called you "an Orthodox Jew." Could you briefly describe your life history and how your relationship with the Lubavitcher Rebbe began?*

HW   I come from a parve background, not religious, not anti-religious, more Labor Zionist. During my college years I was suddenly entranced by the youth Zionist Movement, which led me to an interest in Judaism, beyond and before Zionism. I never had heard of Lubavitch or even Orthodoxy. For some reason at that time I didn't analyze Orthodoxy. I wanted to bring Mitzvoth into my life, event thought I didn't know what the Mitzvoth were.

I knew I had been taught to put on Tefillin when I was Bar Mitzvah, so I decided to resume doing that in my second year. A Rabbi in Boston reminded me how to do it, so that became part of my life. Ever since, I have put on Tefillin, no matter where I have gone. That included on ship in the Second World War, among sailors who were quite appalled by these boxes. This was sort of a test. I failed a few times, but I tried on the whole to do it.

At the end of college I decided that I wanted to study for the Rabbinate. I went to an institution called the Jewish Institute of Religion, which at that time had teachers who covered the spectrum from Orthodoxy to Reform and non-religious.

CD   *Which year was this?*

HW   Just as the war began. I went there for about three years. I was afraid I would not be in the war. It was a different kind of war than the wars we have experienced since. Young people were really afraid of not being included in the war against Hitler. I left Rabbinical school and joined the Marines. I was on the Atlantic for a short time. I was in Amsterdam a short while after the people were freed from the concentration camps, so I saw the Jewish reality at its most compelling and startling stage. I copied down songs that they sang, brought them back to YIVO. While in America, I remember going for Shabbos Friday night to a family there. I remember saying to myself, "To be able to have such a Shabbos after such a holocaust, in a city which had been bombed so thoroughly that you couldn't buy a piece of soap or a piece of string, to have such a Shabbos meant that there was some treasure here."

I went back to school, and I began asking some of the teachers, "Where's the treasure? Where's the thing which has kept us alive. The teachers here are good, I respect them, but I don't find the treasure."

One teacher told me about a teacher of Kabbalah, an old man. I'm now close to his age, but to me he seemed to be hovering at the edge of the grave. Actually, he knew Herzl in his youth. His name was Shin Tzaddik Zetzer, a wonderful man. I called him up to ask to study Kabbalah with him. He hung up the phone and said, "Don't bother me."

I didn't bother him. I called two days later and he said, "Don't bother me." I called a third time and he said, "All right, come down." The only trouble was that coming down meant coming down twelve midnight, because he worked in a little store down in the East Side. They gave him free space between midnight and nine in the morning, so he changed his life around to use the free space, and I changed my life around to be with him. I didn't stay till nine in the morning, but I stayed for a couple of hours, and he introduced me to another world of Judaism.

I wrote an article about him, mainly in order to draw attention to him, because he was very poor, and I was poor too. I couldn't help him. I thought, maybe if the world knew about him they would help him. I gave the article to Commentary magazine, and they printed it, to my surprise. The editor, Eli Cohen surprised me by saying that he didn't like Rabbis in general, but I was a writer. He suggested that I write an article about the Lubavitch movement, which I knew nothing about.

He told me where it was, and I went to 770 Eastern Parkway. This began my voyage. This was in the early fifties, around 1953-54. It was not just an article. I began to study with various people, Rabbi Weinberg, who was on the radio. He was very kind, brought me to his home, and taught me. Finally a meeting was arranged with the Rebbe. I came early in the morning. It was a long meeting. I tried to interrupt several times, because people were waiting outside. It was two or three in the morning, and I thought I was taking up too much time. I rose a couple of times, I thanked him and tried to leave, but he motioned me to sit down. Rabbi Hodakov, who was the secretary, kept on buzzing, but he motioned to ignore the buzzing.

He was evidently curious about a reform rabbi in the reform world.

CD   *Were you a pulpit rabbi at that time?*

HW   I was already a pulpit rabbi, with a very small pulpit here in South Orange. I came here when there were forty families. I should tell you that I wanted Zetzer to be a speaker here. I advertised that at eight or nine on a Thursday night, there would be a lecture on the Zohar, in Yiddish, by Shin Tzaddik Zetzer. Thursday night came, eight o'clock came, and Shin Tzaddik Zetzer and I sat in a room. He began to teach me from the Zohar.

CD   *He was a European Jew?*

HW   He was a Maskil. He wasn't frum, but he told us during our relationship that he had decided to begin to eat kosher. He said, "Pretty soon I'm going to meet the Cordovero, meet the Ari HaKodosh. They all eat kosher. How will I be able to meet with them?"

CD   *Did he tell you where he learned his Kabbalah?*

HW   He studied at a Yeshiva, I don't know which one. He was an enormous scholar. He would say of Dr. Ginsburg at the seminary, "He knows that I know, but he doesn't say anything." He was an autodidact, he studied a great deal by himself. He studied Medieval philosophy. He knew, that the Kabbalah in large part, at least in the Middle Ages, was something which absorbed Medieval Philosophy. Crescas and others were part of the background. This was not known by many people, but he knew it and he used to write articles about it.

He had problems with his teeth, and very often his teeth were out of his mouth. To hide this fact, he would hold a in front of his mouth, and teach me Kabbalah through the handkerchief.

CD   *Going back to the Yechidus.*

HW   I should also mentioned that by that time I had written an article in Commentary Magazine on Rav Kook. To my surprise, the Rebbe knew about everything I had written. We spoke, among other things, about Rav Kook.

Anyway, I went home after two or three hours with the Rebbe. I wrote down my recollections, and I kept on studying with other people in Lubavitch, to become acquainted with the literature of Chabad. I then had a chance for another interview.

CD   *You discussed with the Rebbe your personal desire to learn Kabbalah?*

HW   I didn't stress this. I wanted to know about Lubavitch, about faith in general, questions about which any Jewish young person wants to know. How can you have faith?

I said to the Rebbe, "You say to have faith. Everyone wants to have faith. How do you get faith?" His answer was along the lines of, "Everyone needs food, and everyone eats. But just because you ate yesterday doesn't mean you don't have to eat today. Faith is something which you have to feed, every day." I took it to mean he meant through prayers, through Mitzvoth, you keep on feeding faith.

CD *Right. After leaving Yechidus: First, what one thing stands out, and second, what were your feelings at the end of the night?*

HW First, I was surprised that the Rebbe had the time. Even then, 770 was not as large a center as it later became, there were people waiting from all over the world. I was surprised the Rebbe had taken the time to learn about my own background, and to read stuff I had written, because I knew if he did this for me he did it for everybody. I wondered how he was able to do all that.

Secondly, I was impressed by the quiet, persuasive, gentle but forceful logic of the answers. I saw an individual whose total life was dedicated to that which was outside himself, with no desire of any kind for personal aggrandizement or anything like that.

I asked him about how one becomes Rebbe. Since I was new, I was able to ask questions which were quite Chutzpadik, not knowing they were.

I meant, how does a person suddenly decide that he is a Rebbe? His answer to me was, "What do you do if there's a library of books and someone puts the key in your pocket and walks away?" Later I found out more, the pressures, the hesitations, how it took a year. I began to learn about these things by inquiring.

CD *Did you become a little more of a believer that night?*

HW I became a believer in the teaching that one has to feed faith, that if you don't feed it, it will just evaporate. I believe to this day, that no matter in what condition you are, despair, feeling dried up, feeling it's the end of things, you can't just think it through. You can't just lie there and think, "I wish I were optimistic, I wish I had faith." You have to do something which will nourish you. It can be a mitzvah — prayer becomes to me more and more a means of nourishment. It can be meditation perhaps, but there has to be an active intake of faith.

CD   *The second Yechidus?*

HW   I don't recall the subject of each one, but at one of them I brought my wife. She came in for the second part, if not the whole. This was about a year later. It's interesting that in correspondence later with the Rebbe, he mentioned not only the hope that our meeting would result not only in furtherance of my own religious development, but that these words would also have some effect on my wife.

CD   *What was the discussion with your wife? Was it public, or was it on private issues?*

HW   She is a Litvak. She has a letter from the Rebbe expressing the same sentiments that he wrote to me, hoping she would become more active in Torah and Mitzvos.
       Most of the conversation was with me, and among the subjects, my personal life was only a minor part. He looked upon me as a representative or agent in the non-orthodox world. I knew that he wanted me to be a kind of Shliach to this non-orthodox world. I was convinced enough to assume that role deliberately. When, in the Reform movement, they began arguing against prayer in the public schools, and the Rebbe said prayers were all right, I would get up in the meetings and say, "What's wrong with having prayers?"
       Wherever I had a chance in my own movement, if people would say "Lubavitch is a sect or a cult," I would say to them, "If you would examine historic Judaism, and how Jews acted and looked throughout the ages, and you would look at us, now, what we look like and what we do, if anybody's a cult, we are the cult." I had a chance to do that.

CD   *Did you convince Rabbi Schindler?*

HW   They were open to this. They didn't agree with me, but if they had minds and intellects they could not deny the depths of the

Chabad religious philosophy. Those who knew didn't know much about it. Most of them didn't know much about it. Those who were open to it did understand that they encountered a religious philosophy which was very profound and which could feed them. I was able to become quite accepted in the Reform movement. Maybe they thought of me as someone who was not on the "King's Highway" but they permitted me to say my piece. As time went on, not because of me but because of life itself, more and more people began to wear kipot, to observe Halachah, whatever they called it, and became more open to tradition. Of course, Lubavitch began to grow and to be a major force. Some Reform Rabbis were very much put off by this, but I thought it was wonderful.

The first Yechidus was more about the general philosophy of the Lubavitch movement, about what Rebbe is, what faith is, the function of a Rebbe, and things like that. The second one continued in the same vein, there were just more questions.

CD   *What did the Rebbe have to say about the Holocaust?*

HW   I don't know if it was I who asked the question. I figured that this was a question that everyone asks the Rebbe. What interested me about the Holocaust was the answer of Chabad. I tried to get at that through the study of Chasidus itself. I tried to articulate that answer in the articles I wrote. These articles were not just about the Rebbe himself. They were an attempt to describe the philosophy of Chabad, including its attitude toward evil.

In addition to the personal meetings, there was an active correspondence. At that time I became ill with ulcers and this and that. I felt I had to have an operation, and I wrote to the Rebbe. I got word back immediately, letters and messages, suggesting that I read the Shaar Habitachon in the Chovot Halevovot. He said, "If you have to have the operation it's better to wait until Adar." I waited until Adar and I didn't have the operation.

Every year I received a present of honey cake for Rosh Hashanah. If there was any celebration in my community, there was always a word, by a Shliach or by a written letter.

And I would write to him. Sometimes I would write some

Chutzpedikke questions. Once I wrote, "After telling you about what is going on in my life, I hope you forgive me. I think there is a special bond between us." I should have realized that everyone thinks there is a special bond. I wrote, "I wonder how you are. In the last chapter of my book I quote the remark of the Alter Rebbe to the government official who comes in to visit him. The Alter Rebbe tells him that Hashem asks of everyone, 'Ayeka, Where are you?' May I have the Chutzpah to ask of the Rebbe, 'Ayeka?'"

The Rebbe's reply was wonderful. In general, he said that words that come from the heart enter the heart. If they don't enter the heart, it is a sign they are "Devarim betailim", vain words. If you are asking me how I look upon myself and how I analyze whether my life is a success, I would have to ask you, "What happened to my words?" Did your life change?

He brought the question back to me, and he indicated that that is how he judges himself, and that's how every leader should judge himself. Maybe the words aren't coming out of his heart, and that's why they're not working. He said it in a few words.

In the same letter I asked him about how many orthodox people seem to get caught in this and that crooked deal, etc. He said, "You are making a comparison between the best of the non-religious and the worst of the religious. Why not compare the best of the religious with the best of the non-religious, and the worst of the religious with the worst of the non-religious, and see how the calculation comes out?"

His answers were always direct, pungent like that. Amazingly he took the time to write letters which were long, which had thought in them. He would send them out on time, when I was ill it was by special messenger.

Later on, it became almost impossible to have these long private audiences and long letters, but when there was never a moment I needed something that I couldn't get through to the Rebbe through somebody there.

CD   *Here is a copy of the previous mentioned letter from the Rebbe:*

Greeting and Blessing:

After the long interval, I was pleased to receive your letter of 25th of Teves, though I had inquired about you from time to time through mutual friends. But, of course, indirect information can only be general and superficial and cannot substitute for direct communication.

I appreciate the kind sentiments expressed in your letter. But I am mindful of the dictum of our Sages of the Talmud (B. M. end of p. 84a) to the effect that compliments and approbations, however justified do not help to clarify issues, where as a question or challenge, requiring an answer or explanation, can be more helpful to bring out important practical points and elucidations.

Following this principle and especially in view of the opening lead of your letter, referring to the well-known question (and challenge) Ayeka-where are you- in light of the Alter Rebbe's explanation of it, which reappears again in the concluding paragraph of your letter, the course of my response is already chartered.

There is no need, of course, to point out to you that when the question Ayeka is posed to a private individual, it is likely to refer to the individual personally and to his immediate family, while the same question put to a person of influence and communal responsibility, to whom many look up for inspiration, Chinuch and guidance in their dally life and conduct, the question has much wider implications. It also calls for an assessment as to where he stands and what he has accomplished in the public domain. Indeed, perhaps the latter is the more significant challenge, for it is there that the person's fullest achievement is expressed, as it comes to light in those who benefited from his influence, and it is more significant for many reasons.

Needless to say, the foregoing is not contradicted in the least by the popular adage - "first correct yourself then correct others." Certainly in this country, and in these days, it is the duty of everyone who has any influence in his surroundings to take an active part in promoting Torah-Chinuch, bearing in mind that even a slight improvement during the formative years may well result in significant benefits in later years to the extent of affecting one's whole life and that of one's family, etc. The prospect is not the same, of course, for the person who is of the older generation, since he is already a mature person with a defined course in life, though he, too, is capable of a radical change and advancement to an incomparable degree.

As you are surely aware, the contemporary young generation, more than at any other time in the past, is not afraid of a challenge, even if it should entail radical change and great hardship. It is rather those who are supposed to present the challenge to them who fail to give our youngsters credit, thinking that if it is offered in a diluted form, it will be more appealing and acceptable. Their fear of tofasta miruba [too much at once] has got them down so much that all that they offer is miut sheb'miut-very little- not realizing how self-defeating their approach is.

I should not be at ease with my conscience, both for my sake and yours, if I were not to put it in plain words. I am confident that you will not take it amiss. I speak of living Yiddishkeit in the dally life and conduct in terms of actual observance, what our Sages call maise eikar - the essential thing is the practice of the Mitzvos; not the kind of Judaism that is practiced on certain occasions, or on certain days of the year, but every day; until the habit becomes second nature - in this case, actually the essential nature.

I recall seeing in your book (I believe you also mentioned it to me personally) about your spending some time with the Neturei Karta in Jerusalem. Thus the question Ayeka should include also an appraisal of the distance between them and others in terms of total commitment and dedication. As for some negative aspects which you found there in your estimation, I believe that if a fair assessment is made, one would have to admit that there are more negative aspects in circles of the other extreme.

Now a word about my Ayeka , to which you refer at the end of your letter. Certainly it includes all that has been said above, and more. I wonder what were the "practical" results of our meeting and discussion, with you and your wife, when I was not only a listener but also a speaker. My Ayeka makes me ponder to what extent were my words effective- not in terms of pleasant recollections, but in terms of maise eikar. I will not dwell on this point, not out of any apprehension that it may embarrass you, but because there is no need to elaborate on it to you.

But I do wish to mention another pertinent point, though I may have mentioned it in the course of our conversation. I have in mind the matter of devarim biteilim, "useless words," which, like all expressions of our Sages, is a precise and meaningful term. Whenever we come across this term in Halacha, and even more so in Pnimius haTorah, it is of course in a rather negative and reprehensible sense, and in some respects it has to do with kedushas haloshon, the sanctity of language. At first glance, a more appropriate expression would seem to be devarim asurim, "forbidden words," or devarim miusim," "obscene words," or some similar term as "unbecoming language," and the like. But this is precisely where the meaning of devarim biteilim comes in, namely, that it refers not to the quality of the word, but to their effect, whether they useful or useless. One may speak good words, even quoting words of Torah, but if they do not impress the listener and do not affect him in terms of maise eikar, the deed is primary, then they are devarim biteilim. The blame must be placed on the speaker, since we have the rule that "words coming from the heart penetrate the heart and are eventually effective."

I trust that this letter finds you and your family in good health. If you should think it worthwhile to convey some points of my letter to your wife, I would be gratified, of course.

With blessing, Menachem Schneerson

P.S. After writing the above, I have just your telephone message about the medical treatment suggested by your doctors, and your request for my advice.

It is well known that in a case of an ulcer a very important factor is peace of mind; and this is mainly up to the patient. I therefore suggest that you should strengthen your Bitochon (real trust) in G-d, the Healer of All Flesh Who Works Wondrously. And the way to do it is by reviewing appropriate texts on this subject, such as, for example, Shaar Habitochon in (Ibn Pakuda's) Duties of the Heart, and the like, and reflect deeply on this subject.

*In addition, it is also well known that a suitable diet is help-
ful in such a condition, and I believe helpful in all cases, the difference being only in degree. Hence, in as much as the condition has
been with you for some time, I suggest that you should first give a
try to the above two remedies and see to what extend they can
relieve the situation.*

*In any case, the auspicious month of Adar is only three
weeks away, and in the meantime you can observe the results of the
two measures suggested above. To ease your anxiety sooner, this
letter is being dispatched by Special Delivery.*

*Incidentally, the content of the above letter, though dictated
before your telephone message, may well be the "preemptive cure".
For everything is by Hashgocha Protis, and among human
beings— even non-Jews— there is something that is called "pre-
monition," or, what our Sages describe as niba vlo yoda ma niba-
He prophesized and didn't know that he prophesized.*

CD   *How many letters did you accumulate?*

HW   I must have around six or so. I have to put them together.
When my mother died, he wrote me a letter consisting of three
pages. Page One was brief. It consisted of condolences. Then came
two stenographic long pages, called ps. He said, "In case you wonder why I call this a ps, it's because I don't want you to think I'm
taking advantage of your grief in order to tell you the things I want
to tell you. I want to separate your distress and my desire for your
comfort from what I now have to tell you. Then he explained how
a person should look upon death. Death is a Teshuvah. The essence
of Teshuvah is that it should cause an entire change in a person's
life, not that he goes back and does the same things he was doing
before. That's not Teshuvah. One returns to his one's essence,
which of course has to do with Torah and Mt. What struck me is
that the Teshuvah connected with death should evoke a revolution
in a person. He should be different.

This was very important to me. I used it in my own work,
my preaching. This is a story I never told. Elliot Cohen, who gave
me my first chance in Commentary to be a writer, became

depressed, and he was put in a sanitarium. I went to visit him. He was a young man. I didn't really know what to say to him, but we spoke. He had regrets about some of the attacks on him for the magazine not being Jewish enough. These attacks had evidently gotten to him and it was a part of his depression. I tried to say what I could.

Anyway, after a few months, he went back to work. The doctor said the cure for this kind of depression is to get people back to where they were before, doing the same thing. This is called a cure, in terms of ordinary medical experience, that you should go back and sit behind the same desk and function properly.

So they did that, they "cured" him that way, but a few months later he committed suicide. I was at the funeral. I never forgot that, that what a person needs at a certain time in life is not at all to go back to where he is. He needs a revolution to occur. What Elliot Cohen, it seemed to me, needed , was something altogether different, a big change.

CD   *You used the Rebbe's idea in a practical way.*

HW   And I've used it ever since, for myself, because I think it's true. Maimonides says that death means that a person should do Teshuvah. I've used the Rebbe's teachings in my work all the time. I translated them into my terminology, which my people could understand.

CD   *So that three-page letter was all about the meaning of death. With your permission, I will print it as part of the interview.*

HW   Sure. The letter explains the spiritual meaning of death, and also practical advice about what to study, which Mishnas to read and things like that. I published parts of that letter, and I always get inquiries from people who are interested in knowing these things. I always get a positive response. The Rebbe's words to me were always of use to large, large circles, and my own life became more and more integrated with Chasidus. I studied with HaRav Steinsalz in Jerusalem. He taught Chabad literature all the time, and I tried to study and understand it and to write about it. To this day I keep up my connections.

CD   *Here is the part of the letter which the Rebbe sent him after his mother's passing:*

On the basis of our personal acquaintance, and what I have heard about you from mutual friends, I take the liberty of suggesting to you that in addition to Kaddish at the daily prayers, followed by Kaddish d'rabonon after Mishnayos, as is customary, you also include learning a practical Halacho, such as from the Kitzur Shulchon Oruch. This is of special importance in our day and age, and it has many worthwhile implications. Above all, it is a Zechus Horabim, coupled with a special Zechus for the soul of the departed. Also, furthering adherence to the Will of G-d, especially by a person of influence, gives practical expression to Yisgadal v'Yiskadash Shmei Rabba.

I also wish to make a further point in the light of Chasidus, which gives a new insight into the concept of Teshuvoh. Teshuvoh, as interpreted in Chasidus, does not mean "repentance" (which is only one aspect of it), but as the word indicates - a return of the soul to its "source and root." The "return" referred to here is not the return of the soul to its Maker at the end of its allotted years on earth, but its return to its true essence. As explained by the Alter Rebbe in his Tanya, chapter 31, this is achieved when the Jew is engaged in Torah and Mitzvos, especially when it is permeated with inner joy and inspiration. For at that time, too, the soul "departs from the body," in the sense that it abandons the bodily needs, inclinations and lusts. Moreover, at such time the soul actually involves the body in the spiritual exercise, inducing it, too, to obey the Will of G-d, the Source of the soul and of all existence, so that not only the soul returns to its Source, but it also takes the physical body along with it.

The above provides an insight into what seems to be a somewhat "incongruous" observation by the Rambam, namely, that the period of mourning observed by a bereaved family has to do with Teshuvoh. [And it is written, "But the living shall take it to heart."] One would expect that the first natural reaction of a person sustaining such a loss would be that of resentment and complaint. However, in the light of what has been said above, it is understandable why, on deeper reflection, the shock of seeing a dear soul depart this life should induce Teshuvoh. For this is a fitting time to reflect upon the opportunities which have been given to the soul to "return" to its Source while it is here on earth, housed in its body, and in this experience of Teshuvoh to live a meaningful and happy life to a ripe old age. I trust there is no need for further elaboration on the above to you.

A word of explanation. This entire piece has been written as a ps and on a separate sheet, not because it is of lesser importance than the letter preceding it. [On the contrary?] However, our Sages wisely reminded us that allowances should be made for a person in distress. The thought might just occur that here comes a man, who is not a relative, and wishes to take advantage of a profound and unhappy experience in order to advance his ideals. For this reason this part of the letter has been separated from the first. But in truth the two parts are not really separate but intimately connected. Besides, and this is the main point: these ideals are not only mine, but (also?) yours. To quote the Alter Rebbe again, "a Jew neither desires nor is capable of being separated from G-dliness." Only circumstances sometimes obscure the truth." I believe with com- plete faith" that this is the way to gratify the soul which is in the World of Truth, and I venture to say that you also share this belief.

May G-d grant that henceforth you will actualize the above by the stimulus of happy occasions, in accordance with the contents of the said chapter in Tanya, through the study of our Torah, Toras Emes, the kind of study that leads to action, the fulfillment of the Mitzvos in the daily life. And may you together with your wife bring up your children in this spirit. I refer not only to your natural children, but also to your "children" figuratively speaking, namely, those who look up to you as teacher and mentor, as our Sages interpret the words, "And thou shalt teach them diligently unto thy children" - "thy students."

CD   *I saw a picture of you, going with Rabbi Bogomilsky, to receive a dollar from the Rebbe. Was there anything special at that time?*

HW   Yes, it was only a few months before the Rebbe got ill. I went several times to receive a brocha, and dollars for my grandchildren, and so forth. This time, I was introduced again to the Rebbe, (Around the time that the Rebbe stopped having private one on one Yechidus meetings I ceased to correspond with the Rebbe.) I had the second edition of my book. The Messianic fervor had begun to grow at that time. When I was introduced again, I said I was the author of 9 1/2 Mystics. The Rebbe said, "9 1/2 is a good number, but it's not enough. It should be ten, whole and complete. I want you to announce in the very synagogue where you have operated that you are an orthodox Jew, and that you always have been an orthodox Jew, even though you have served as a Rabbi in a Reform Temple, and I would like you to publicly announce it." I have a video of that.

I didn't know what to say, so I put my hand on my heart and said, "I put your words on my heart."

Then, at my 75th birthday I was honored at the temple for my forty years as Rabbi. (The last few years I'm Rabbi Emeritus). The Temple made a celebration. I said to myself, here I am standing at the pulpit. I said, "I have something to announce." I told about the Rebbe, and what he had said to me, and so forth. So I said, "Even though I have served in a reform pulpit, in my heart I have always been orthodox, and I am fulfilling the request of the Rebbe." The celebration went on and no one said anything at all to me about my comment. I was surprised by the lack of interest. I thought that right after I made that comment, people would come to me and say, "Oh really" or "Why?" However, to my disappointment, not a word!

Later on, during the party, people made speeches, and were reminiscing. One very nice former president got up and said, "Oh yes, Rabbi, about that announcement. We always knew you are an Orthodox Jew. It is all right, we always knew that."

That was my last formal exchange with the Rebbe.

CD   *In all your years with the Rebbe, did you ever discuss the idea of Moshiach?*

HW   No, I do not think we ever had any discussion. I never suspected from any discussions that the Rebbe had Messianic aspirations.

CD   *Not the Rebbe himself, but the general idea.*

HW   At every farbrengen, I always felt that the Rebbe told us that we were living not in ordinary days, but that this was a coming together of historic events, of happenings which were unique, and that such enormous happenings as the letting go of the Jews from Russia, the establishment of the state of Israel, these were all indications of the greater moment of whatever you want to call it, the Messianic moment was approaching very close. This I think I heard every Sicha. The Rebbe believed it. It was definitely not said just as a formality. These are those days.
          In the second edition of my book I had to respond to all these current questions about Moshiach.

CD   *You made a reference to when the Rebbe became ill?*

HW   When the Rebbe became ill it seemed to me that something had to be said, to be written for the outside world. The non-Messianic world, the world outside, was more or less mocking these outcries. People were also saying that the Lubavitcher movement was finished, that this was the end, and I was hearing from Lubavitcher people also that there would be no more Rebbes.

CD   *This was before the Rebbe's passing.*

HW   Yes, at the time the Rebbe was ill. So I was asked by a number of people. CNN called me up and asked me to appear. I appeared two or three times and tried to explain to people who were not at all involved what was meant by Moshiach. Someone had made a video and it kept appearing over and over on Channel 13. I was able to say a word about Moshiach which I think was of some little help.

CD   *What did you say?*

HW   Briefly, you have to understand that Moshiach is not some magic thing. It is the hope that everyone has in his heart, Jew or non-Jew. Does anybody want their children to be involved in wars again and again? Is there anybody who is not dreaming of a time when there won't be any more wars, when there won't be this terrible fighting and hating? Doesn't everyone have that hope in his heart. That's the Messianic hope, that's all it is. There will be a catalyst, a catalytic agent, who will bring that kind of a jump, a jump in consciousness, into being. That catalytic agent is called the Moshiach. This is not something absurd, something crazy.

Forgive my immodesty, but I think this helped even the Lubavitcher Chasidim. The Messianic hope is not a strange hope. Everybody shares in it, someplace in their heart. That there can be a person, or an agent of some sort, who somehow makes the jump, there are many leaders who create jumps in consciousness. Our history is filled with leaders who brought about huge changes. There's nothing strange, and I believe this.

The second thing is that I believed, and I still believe, that the Lubavitcher movement is not finished with the passing of the Rebbe. It doesn't depend on some sort of rising or some sort of Messianic appearance. If it happens, it's G-d's mystery, but I don't think that Lubavitch depends for its future on that. I base that, maybe incorrectly, on something the Rebbe said to me in one of the interviews I've written about. In my first interview I asked the Rebbe, "This whole movement, everything that's happening here, depends on the Rebbe. What is a Rebbe?" He gave me an answer, a very nice answer. Then I said, "It depends upon you, on the Rebbe." His answer to me was, "I'm not so sure." At that time I just wrote it down. I thought it was just modesty. I looked again at it last year. I said to myself, "The Rebbe didn't just say words, he always said words which had content to them." When he said, "I'm not so sure that this movement cannot live without me, or perhaps even without a Rebbe," maybe there was something in that. I may be wrong, but I still think about it, and I have a heretical thought.

Sometimes I think there were prophets, and prophecy ceased at a certain point. There were Rebbes, magnificent Rebbes. It can be that Ruach Hakodesh takes different vessels to speak to us. Prophets once, Rabbis another time, Rebbes another time. Who knows? This may be the seventh Rebbe. Perhaps now there's another type of leadership that has to take over the teachers of Lubavitch etc. It's hard for me to say. All I know is that Lubavitch has a life and a teaching to offer which is not around in other places. It is one of the most, profound, nourishing religious... I don't know what to call it. It's religious nourishment on its deepest and highest level.

I think it's needed, and that it will keep on offering itself. If you want to call it the spirit of the Rebbe, I believe in the spirit of the Rebbe. If you want to call it the spirit of all the Rebbes of Chasidism, fine. If you want to say it is Moshe Rabbeinu, and the Rebbe is another Moshe at Sinai, fine. Whatever it is, it's got a future.

I see that there is activity and growth and the Shluchim are out there working, sometimes the demand creates the response. There is a great demand for Lubavitch. I have high hopes. I think it is needed, and if it continues to bring forth new fruit, it can be the Rebbe acting through us, why not, whatever it is. That's my hope.

CD *In a sense you were a close friend of the Rebbe. He treated you like a son. How do you personally feel? Our father has left the physical world. As a friend and a child, how do you take that?*

HW I feel greatly in debt to the Rebbe. For me it is easier than for real Lubavitcher Chasidim. I was not brought up with the need of a Rebbe, bringing everything to the Rebbe and receiving the blessing and feeling weak if the blessing wasn't there, feeling out in the ocean if I didn't get that blessing. I don't come from that background. I understand the meaning of it. I wanted to get the Brocho myself when I had a problem. So I understand the meaning of the Brocho. But I've lived a lot of life outside of it, so it's much easier for me.

My hope is that the wonderful people who have been true to Lubavitch, which is the fruit of a wonderful tree. It doesn't just go back to the Alter Rebbe, it comes from way, way back. That that fruit will send down roots into the soil from which the Rebbe himself grew, and somehow make a transformation. I think it's going to take a lot of time for that. Whether another person will come along, I don't think this is even necessary to talk about, because it is too artificial, too business-like. If a person comes along, he will come along. Meanwhile, there is no answer other than what the Rebbe gave me, as to how to confront death. I look at what the Rebbe wrote — teshuvah, meaning returning to the mitzvoth and to study, with simcha, always besimcha, and this kind of a return will give a future to Lubavitch.

I go everyplace. I took a cruise a few months ago. I went to Alexandria, to the big Sefardic synagogue there. There's the Lubavitcher Rebbe's picture! Anywhere I go, if I need to find a friend, spend a Shabbos, I know there's Lubavitch. I know that it has to be maintained.

Suggested Readings

1.   Likutei Amarim (Tanya), Rabbi Shneur Zalman, Bilingual Edition, Kehot:1973

2.   Memoirs, by Rabbi Joseph I. Schneerson, Translated by Nissan Mindel. Vol. I-II. Kehot: 1956, 1960

3.   On The Essence of Chasidus, Rabbi Menachem Mendel Schneerson, translated by Rabbi Hershel Greenberg, Kehot:1986

4.   Likkutei Dibburim, by Rabbi Yosef Yitzchok Schneerson, translated by Uri Kaploun, Vol. 1-3, Kehot:1987-1990

5.   Timeless Patterns in Time, Rabbi Menachem M. Schneerson, translated by Rabbi Eliyahu Touger, Vol. 1, Kehot:1993

6.   Torah Studies, by Rabbi M. M. Schneerson, adapted by Rabbi Jonathan Sacks, Lubavitch Foundation:1986

7.   Philosophy of Chabad, by Nissan Mindel, Vol. 1 and 2, Kehot:1973

8.   Likutei Sichos, Rabbi Menachem Mendel Schneerson, Vol. 1-39, Kehot: 1996

9.   Letters by the Lubavitcher Rebbe (English), 1950-78, Vaad L'Hafotzas Sichos, 1979

10.   Igrot Kodesh (Yiddish, Hebrew), 1928-65 [collected correspondence of the Rebbe], 25 volumes, Kehot: 1987-95

GLOSSARY

Ahavas Yisroel: loving one's fellow Jew

Aibeshter: G-d

Alter Rebbe, the (lit., "the Old Rebbe"): Rabbi Shneur Zalman of Liadi (1745-1812), the founder of the Chabad-Lubavitch trend within the Chasidic movement; author of the Tanya, a classic text of the Chasidic tradition, and Shulchan Aruch HaRav, a classic legal code

Amida: The "Standing service"; also known as the silent prayer. It is the central prayer of the prayer service; Also called the "Shemoneh Esreh-the "Eighteen [blessings]

Avoda (lit. "Service"): formerly, the sacrificial service in the Temple, and later, the service of prayer instituted in its stead

Arizal (lit., "the lion of blessed memory"): acronym for R. Issac Luria (1534-1572), one of the leading luminaries of the Kabbalah

Baal Shem Tov, the (lit., "Master of the Good Name"): Rabbi Yisroel ben Eliezer (1698-1760), founder of the Chasidic movement

Beis HaMikdash: the (First or Second) Temple in Jerusalem

Ben Bayis: Like a son in his house

Chabad (acronym for the Hebrew words meaning "wisdom, understanding, and Knowledge"): the approach to Chasidism which filters its spiritual and emotional power through the intellect; a synonym for Chabad is Lubavitch, the name of the town where this movement originally flourished

Chacham: Wise person

Chasid (pl. Chasidim): A pious person; specifically, the term is used to refer to a follower of a Chasidic holy man (Rebbe, Tzaddik) and a member of the Chasidic movement of the Baal Shem Tov

Chasidus, Chasidism: Chasidic thought

Chazer Chasidus: To Repeat or Recite a Chasidic discourse one has heard.

Chazon: Cantor

Chinuch: lit. "Dedication" or "education"

Chinuch Atzmai: Educational system run by religious party

Cheder (pl., chadarim): school in which young children learn reading skills and begin the study of Torah

Chok Mihu Yehudi: The Who Is A Jew Law

Chutzpah: Impudence, brazenness

Dati: (lit., "Religious") Orthodox; observant Jew

Davven (v): to pray; davvening (n): Jewish prayer

D'vekus: Cleaving to G-d

Elokim: The Name of G-d that represents Divine Justice

Emuna: faith

Eretz Yisroel: Land of Israel

Erev: Eve. Generally used for the daylight hours before a holy day, as for example: Erev Shabbos

Gan Eden: Paradise

Gaon: A title denoting exceptional rabbinic learning and genius

Gadol(ei) Hador: Greatest (great) Torah schalor (s) of generation

Gehenim: Purgatory

Halachah (pl., halachos): (a) the body of Torah law; (b) a particular law

Hashem: Literally, "The Name" (the four-letter Name of G-d that can't be uttered); this is a way of referring to G-d

Hava'ye: The four-letter Name of G-d

Kabbalah (lit., "received tradition"): the Jewish mystical tradition

Kabbalas ol (lit., "the acceptance of G-d's yoke"): an unsweyvering, selfless commitment to doing the Will of G-d

Kaddish: A prayer said during the synagogue prayer service. There are a number of forms, the most well known being the one recited as a memorial for the dead

Kavvanah: The intention directed toward G-d while performing a religious deed. Can also mean a particular intention (for a prayer); the plural in that usage is kavvanos

Kedusha: A responsive prayer said during the synagogue service, when the prayer leader repeats the Amida

Korbonos: Sacrifices

Kos Shel Brocho: Cup of blessing, referring to the cup of wine used for religious purposes

Leshem Shomayim: For the sake of G-d

Likkutei Dibburim: a selection of the public talks of the sixth Lubavitcher Rebbe, Rabbi Yosef Yitzchok Schneerson

Maamar: a formal Chasidic discourse

Maarach: Labor party

Mamash: Literally

Mamlachet Dati: Israel's governmental educational system

Mechitzo(s): Divider in the synagouge seperating men and women

Mesiras Nefesh (lit., sacrifice of the soul"): the willingness to sacrifice oneself, either through martyrdom, or through a selfless life, for the sake of the torah and its commandments

Midrash: classical collection of the sages' homiletic teachings on the Torah

Mikveh: a ritual bath used by women for purification after emerging from the state of niddah (spiritual impurity) and used by both men and women in their endeavors to attain spiritual self-refinement

Min Hashomayim: Literally "from Heaven" referring to G-d

Mincha: The daily afternoon prayer service

Minyon: The minimum prayer quorum of ten

Mishnah: Ancient collection of legal; decisions of the sages; the earliest part of the Talmud, it's the text to which the Talmud is the commentary.

Misiras Nefesh: Self Sacrifice for G-d, Judaism, and Torah

Misnagid (pl. Misnagdim): An opponent of the Chasidic movement of the Baal Shem Tov

Mizrachi: Religious Zionists

Moshiach: lit., "the anointed one"): the Messiah

Moshe Rabbeinu (lit., "Moses our teacher"): the "father of the prophets," who redeemed the Jews from Egypt and brought them to the revelation at Mount Sinai

Musar: Chastisement; Ethical teachings

Neshomo: Soul

Ohel: Lit. "tent", refers to the graveside of the Rebbe and previous Rebbe.

Parshas: the Torah Portion of [a certain Shabbos of festive occasion]

Previous Rebbe: Rabbi Yosef Yitzchok Schneerson (1880-1950)

Reb: A Title of respect; Mister

Rambam (acronym for Rabbi Moshe ben Maimon; 1135-1204): Maimonodies, one of the foremost Jewish thinkers of the middle ages; wrote the Mishne Torah, Guide for the Perplexed, etc.

Rashi (acronym for Rabbi Shlomo Yitzchaki;1040-1105):the author of the foremost commentary to the Torah and the Talmud

Rebbe (lit., "my teacher [or master]"): saintly Torah leader who serves as spiritual guide to a following of Chasidim

Rosh (Ha)Yeshiva: Dean of a Yeshiva, (lit., "sitting", referring to an academy of Torah studies in which one of the principal methods of learning is dialogue between students to discover the meaning of the teachers' lectures and the underlying texts.)

Rov: Rabbi

Sefer: (pl. seforim) Jewish holy books

Shabbos: the Sabbath

Shabbos HaGodol: The Shabbos before Passover

Shechinah: the Divine Presence

Shliach: (pl. Shluchim) (lit. Messenger) Emmisary, in Chabad, this refers to the Rebbe's emmisaries throughout the world

Shlomo: King David's son and successor, who built the First Temple in the tenth century

Shulchan Aruch: the standard Code of Jewish law compiled by Rabbi Yosef Caro in the mid-sixteenth century

Sivan: the third month of the Jewish year

Talmid (pl. Talmidim): Disciple, student

Talmud: The sixty volumes of Jewish law, expounding upon the Torah. It is comprised of the Mishne and the (later) discussion and commentary, based on the mishneh , called the Gemara. The terms Talmud and Gemara are used interchangeably

Tanya: the classic text of Chabad Chasidic thought authored by Rabbi Shneur Zalman of Liadi

Techiyas Hameisim: Ressurection of the dead

Tehillim (lit., "praises"): the Book of Psalms, authored by King Dovid

Teshuva (lit., "return [to G-d]"): repentance

Thirteen Attributes of Mercy: G-d's boundless capacity for compassion, especially as expressed in the granting of atonement

Tifillin: small leather boxes each containing four Torah passages which the Torah commands adult males to wear daily during the morning prayers

Tisch: The public Shabbos and holiday meals at the table of chasidic Rebbes, where the Rebbe says words of Torah and the chasidim sing songs and toast l'chaim

Torah: The five of Moshe; the Tanach (acronym for Torah, Niveim, and Kesuvim, five books of Moshe, Prophets, and the Writings); or, more broadly, all Jewish writings throughout the ages

Torah Umada: Judaism via both religious and secular studies.

Tzaddik (pl. Tzaddikim): A righteous or holy person; leader of a Chasidic group, a Rebbe

Tzedaka: Charity

Yeshiva: Rabbinical Academy

Yetzer Hara: Evil inclination

Yetzer Tov: Good inclination

Yichidus: Private Audience with the Rebbe

Yichudim: Unifications, in a technical sense, usually a kabbalistic meditation on one of the letter configurations of the four -letter name of G-d.; the unity of G-d that's accomplished through the performance of mitzvos

Yiddishkeit: Judaism

YHVH: The special Name of G-d; also called the "four-letter name," the four English letters standing for the Hebrew letters Yud Hey Vav Hey

Zecher: Remembrence

Zemirot: Devotional Shabbos table songs

Zitz: Sit down

Zohar: The "Book of Splendor", the central book of the Kabbalah, the Jewish mystical tradition, authored by Rabbi Shimon Bar (ben) Yechai (2nd century)

Zt"l: Acronym for Zechrono Tzaddik Levrocho, may the memory of the tzaddik be remembered

RESOURCE MATERIALS
FROM THE AUTHOR

1
Your Better Self
A Guide to Self-Improvement Based on Chasidic Teachings
US$15

2
Demystifying the Mystical
Understanding the Language and Concepts of
Chasidism and Jewish Mysticism - A Primer for the Layman
US$25.00

3
To Be Chasidic: A Contemporary Guide
US $30

4
Audio Cassettes - Chabad Niggunim Series; Learn, Understand & Sing
1. Actualize Your Higher Soul - (Awe, Commitment, Depth)
2. Actualize Your Deeper Soul - (Pleasure, Feelings, Inner-Self)
3. Actualize Your Better Soul - (Trust, Belief, Security)
4. Actualize Your Happiness - (Happiness, Strength, Anticipation)
US$10 each, US$35 set of 4 tapes

5
Video Cassette - Your Better Self
Part One - Farbrengen
Part Two - Niggunim
US$15

(Please add US$5 shipping & handling)

send check or money order to
JEC Publishing
821 N. Formosa Ave., #202
Los Angeles, CA 90046
(213) 954-1770

222

SPONSORS

In honor of
Gavriel Yosef's Bar Mitzvah

28 Nissen 5756 - April 17, 1996

Yakov Yitzchok, Yehudit, Eliyohu Bentzion,
Doniel Avrohom Dalfin
Costa Rica, Central America

May you grow up to be a Chasid, Yiras Shomayim, and
Lamden
May you bring Yiddishe and Chasidishe nachas to your
parents and Klal Yisroel

Mendel Duchman
Yakov and Esther Ginsburg
Dalia Goldfarb
In Honor of Nicholas Heiman
In Honor of Mendel (the "soldier") and Sima Greenbaum

Mordechai, Alex, and Eli Kahan and family,
brocho for parnoso tova biharchovo

In Loving Memory of Rabbi Berel Levy

Lezak Family, in honor of the Geula
Sidney Priegel
Zev and Varda Rav-Noy
Gregg and Marcia Small, for a healthy baby

Moshe Aron, Rutie, and Sholom Eliezer Weiss, Sherman Oaks, CA
Lionel and Malka Zucker and family

In Memory
of our
Dear and Beloved Grandparents

Shluchim of the Previous Rebbe and the
Rebbe to
Melbourne, Australia

Harav Hagaon v'Hachosid
Reb Yehoshua Schneur Zalman

8 Teves -Gimmel Tammuz
1905 - 1991

and

A Woman of Valor and Modesty
Brocho

Adar - 8 Teves
1905 - 1987

Serebryanski

In Loving Memory of our parents

Mr. Chaim Bentzion and Mrs. Miriam
Viroslav

and
our sister

Anita Viroslav

by

Samuel and Beatrice Viroslav

San Jose, Costa Rica

In Loving Memory of
Abraham and Rochel Weisleder
by
Jeffrey and Sandra Weisleder

In Honor of Mr. and Mrs. Jose and Ester Daniel
In Honor of Mr. and Mrs. Morris and Elaine Zimmerman
by
Luis L. Daniel